T0128817

POSITIONED
for PURPOSE

How to position yourself with God to live the
abundant life that God has destined for you.

TY JONES

WestBow
PRESS
A DIVISION OF THOMAS NELSON

Unless otherwise noted, all Scripture references in this book are taken from the *New King James Version,* © 1982 by Thomas Nelson.

WestBow Press books may be ordered through booksellers or by contacting:

WestBow Press
A Division of Thomas Nelson
1663 Liberty Drive
Bloomington, IN 47403
www.westbowpress.com
1 (866) 928-1240

ISBN: 978-1-4908-1129-1 (sc)
ISBN: 978-1-4908-1130-7 (hc)
ISBN: 978-1-4908-1128-4 (e)

Library of Congress Control Number: 2013918426

Printed in the United States of America.

WestBow Press rev. date: 03/06/2014

DEDICATION

I dedicate this book to the glory and honor of my Savior Jesus Christ, whom I met June 22, 1972 and has continually through His word and indwelling of the Holy Spirit been POSITIONING me into sonship with my Heavenly Father.

I want to thank my beautiful wife, Lou Ann, for being such an encourager to me during the writing of this book. Also to greatest people on earth, the body of Arena of Life church for encouraging me to write this book, and my daughter Brooke who spent countless hours helping to organize the material for the publishers.

ENDORSEMENTS

Pastor Ty Jones has skillfully answered critical questions that sum up the dilemma of man – *Who am I? And, Why am I?* It has been said, *'Your destiny is not yours to decide. It is yours to discover'.* As you examine the valuable revelatory truths in *POSITIONED FOR PURPOSE* you will embark on the discovery of a lifetime. The ever present internal nagging search for man's significance is brought to a divine rest as the reader explores the pages of this book. This is a must read for those who have a burning desire to do more than merely exist. Pastor Ty Jones places tools in your hands to equip you for the search of hidden spiritual riches that will unlock your tomorrows. Embrace your season to be *Positioned for Purpose.*

Scott Coon
Founder & Director Global Connections International

It's an honor for me to recommend *Positioned for Purpose* by my good friend, Pastor Ty Jones. For years I have taught about the importance of a man in our society, knowing that when a man changes, his family will follow him and change also. If there is one thing our culture needs today, it is the desperate need for men to stand up and take their rightful place and responsibility in their family and community. Pastor Jones addresses that in this timely book with clarity and wisdom. It is a powerful call to men everywhere to get in position and assume their godly roles. I believe this book is a must-read for everyone who wants to see a change in our nation: It starts with a change in men.

Mike Barber
President, Mike Barber Ministries

In his book Positioned for Purpose, Pastor Ty Jones gives us a refreshing look at a truth that may be just what you need to be in position to receive the fullness of blessings that our heavenly Father, through Jesus Christ has destined for His own. This is a practical book, born out of experience and shared with warmth and clarity.

Dr. Ronnie Trice
Maranatha Church
Mont Belvieu, TX

INTRODUCTION

On any given Friday night, Saturday or Sunday afternoon there will be 22 young men on a playing field 100 yards in length with goal lines on each end. Each teams ultimate goal for the allotted time for the game is to cross the goal line more times than their opponent. Each team has practiced, probably daily for weeks in preparation for game day. They not only memorize plays from their coaches' playbooks, but they practice these plays until they hopefully have them perfected to the point that they will execute them successfully on the playing field. Each player has been designated a position. The team's success will be determined by their being in the proper position on each play. For instance the quarterback, who calls each play, many times from the coach on the sideline who is strategizing their offensive attack to cross the goal line, leads the offense team. The team on the defensive side has also practiced specially designed plays to counter every scenario they think the other team might use to score. For every play, each of the 11 men has a particular assignment or position. If for instance it is a passing play the one who is to receive or catch the pass thrown from the quarterback would have a preplanned route in which he was to run. Maybe this play would require him to run down the sidelines until he reached the 20-yard line then turn towards the center of the field where the quarterback would throw him the football. Some of the player's position would be to protect the quarterback; others would be to block for the receiver or to be in a designated place on the field in case the opposing safety or linebacker covered to the designated receiver tightly. If all goes well the receiver catches the ball and outruns the defenders into the end zone scoring a touchdown. If any player fails to be in his assigned position, it might cause the plan to go awry.

Victory in every sport is often determined by being in the proper position. The first baseman in baseball would not be successful in tagging out a runner if he decided he wanted to stand on 2nd base. The batter would never hit a homerun if he stood outside the batter's box. The tennis player would win very few matches if they stood continually at the net. I am an avid golfer and I know that in matter of seconds of the golf swing, my hands, arms, legs and torso all must be in the proper position throughout the swing if I am going to strike the ball correctly. Jokingly, I've heard that a golfer had to execute 100 different things during a golf swing, hopefully that's not true.

Life is not a game of chance, but I believe there is something about being in the right place at the right time. Many successful people will tell you that their success was proper timing. Timing is in fact a position. The God of creation didn't just haphazardly sling the stars into heaven. He carefully positioned each one into its' proper place. He positioned all the planets of this universe and also other galaxies as well. As God created each plant and species of the animal kingdom, I believe that He positioned them where they would prosper and flourish. He didn't put the cactus in the artic or the Plumeria tree in the desert areas.

God not only loves you beyond your wildest imaginations, but God is interested in every aspect of your life. God wants you to be successful in life and all that life contains. He so desires for you to be successful that He has a book written about you with chapters for each season of your life. (Psalm 139:16) Like the coach's playbook God has a playbook or plan for your life. Jeremiah 29:11 (NIV) "For I know the plans I have for you," declares the LORD, "plans to prosper you and not to harm you, plans to give you hope and a future." The only difference between the coach's playbook and God's plan is the coach's plan is dependent upon each player being in their proper position and carrying out their assignment. God's success plan for our lives is contingent upon our being in proper position with Him, to receive what He has for us.

This book is to help you to locate that position, get into it and remain in position and live the victorious and overcoming life that is part of your inheritance.

Table of Contents

Chapter 1

PREDESTINED FOR A PURPOSE

My mother tells the story about a time when I was four or five years old. I went with my maternal grandparents to an Easter Sunday service at the Methodist church in our small, west Texas town. I sat between the two of them, eating hard candy that my granddad seemed to have an unending supply of in his pockets. I loved spending time with my grandparents and realized later that my new life in Christ was birthed through their prayers and love of God.

The Easter message must have made an impression on me, because a few weeks later, I tried preaching to my first audience: a litter of puppies. I put the puppies in my red American Flyer wagon and parked it under the elm tree in our backyard. I perched myself on a wooden box I'd found in the garage and began to preach with the fervor of a Pentecostal preacher. All the while my mom, who was hidden from my sight, listened and laughed.

My granddad was quite a character. He loved telling me stories about cowboys and Indians. His passion besides his family was trading horses and cattle; much of my childhood was spent in livestock auctions. It seemed he always had a horse he wanted make sure was "kid broke." Often we saddled our horses and went on long rides. We'd tell stories along the way—stories so vivid they became reality in the mind of a young child. Sometimes we were on the trail after some bad guys or riding as fast as we could, trying to outrun the Apache Indians that were chasing us to scalp us. Those times with him stirred up the natural gift in me to rodeo and trade horses and cattle.

I wish I could say that Easter Sunday changed my life so dramatically that I was saved, went through school, and joined the ministry. But for many years, my life was far from that. I was an only child, and my parents gave me everything I desired. My dad, who had a very dysfunctional life growing up, was unchurched; therefore, church was a foreign thing to me. Our Sundays were consumed with hunting, working on projects around the home, or playing golf at the country club. In contrast to my father, my mother was raised in a very godly home. Later I found out that she was saved as young child at a Christmas Eve service.

I was raised with the notion that some people went to church and some didn't, and we were a family that didn't. I became a very rebellious teenager, getting in trouble constantly in school and at home. My weekends were consumed with heavy drinking. This eventually led to me taking alcohol from my father's liquor cabinet, pouring it into a Mason jar, and drinking it each morning before my first period class in high school. I graduated by the skin of my teeth; I think the principal gave me a diploma just to get rid of me.

I went away to college and was free to live my life beyond my parents' control. I remember filling out college applications. When asked what religion I was, I checked the only religion I had heard of— Christian—even though I'd never thought about being any particular religion. My only desire for college was to rodeo and party. If I had been graded for those two activities, I would have earned an A+. The first semester, I got kicked out for selling liquor on campus to an undercover police officer.

I went on to attend two more colleges, and my life seemed to drift further down the tube. I never thought about God or whether there was a God. The only mental image I had of Jesus was the baby in the manger in Christmas nativity scenes. For some unknown reason, I hated church or anyone who went to church.

But then I had a God encounter in 1972. It was a time when my life was so messed up I felt I had no way out. I was so miserable inwardly that I cried out to God one night, not even knowing if there was a God. I asked Him to change my life, because I had failed every time I tried. That night, I was lying in a ranch-house bed in the bottom of a canyon. God began to show me how me how rebellious I had been my entire life. I began to cry out, asking God to forgive me for all the bad things I had done and for all the people I had hurt.

The next morning, I walked out of my house and saw my friends saddling their horses to help me work cattle that day. I stopped and sat down on the fender of my trailer, out of sight from my friends, and said, "God, I cannot change my life, so our deal is off." But God had done something supernatural that night: He had changed my life, and I've never been the same since.

After I had been kicked and run over several times by the cattle, a Mexican man who worked for me asked, "What's the matter with you? You no getty mad no more." I realized then that all the hate and rage I had inside me had gone, along with the desire for the lifestyle that had been destroying me.

I had no knowledge of the Bible or God, so I called the only preacher I knew, one whom I had ridiculed and cussed at on numerous occasions. I told him I needed to talk. I knew from the very beginning that God had called me to preach the gospel, but I wanted to ignore it. I finally agreed under my terms, which led to Bible studies in our homes.

Finally in 1999, some forty-five years after I preached to those puppies, I said, "God, I want to fulfill the purpose and destiny that You have for me." *Purpose* is defined as "the reason for which something is done or created or for which something exists." Everything in creation has a purpose; trying to change what it was created for will not work. Lawn mowers and snow blowers are both powered by small gasoline engines, but it would be useless to use a lawn mower to remove snow from a driveway and ridiculous to try to mow grass with a snow blower. It's the same thing with people.

The God of creation created you with a purpose and has a plan for your life (Jeremiah 29:11). That is what this book is all about: finding your purpose and staying there fulfilling all that you were created to be.

Many people wander aimlessly through life, trying to find the right person, attain the right goal, or find the right thing to fulfill them. They think, *If only I could find that one person that would fulfill all my needs, then I would be happy.* That is why adultery and divorce are at an all-time high in America. That is why many entertainers and athletes reach a pinnacle in their careers, only to find themselves empty again, often succumbing to addiction or turning to suicide. We believe that if we could have the right thing, we would be happy. So we sacrifice our homes trying to earn enough to buy that thing, only to find out we soon tire of it, and we need a new thing to make us happy. We become like the proverbial dog chasing its tail until stress wears out our bodies and debt overwhelms us—just trying to find purpose in a thing. True happiness is a fleeting thing.

Ecclesiastes 3:1–2 says, "To everything there is a season, / A time for every purpose under heaven." *Season* is the Hebrew word *zeman*, which means "an appointed occasion." Many people wish they could have been born during a different era. But you weren't born a minute too late or a minute too early. In fact, you were born at the perfect time, the beginning of your season. The conditions of your conception don't matter: whether from the desire to produce a child, an illicit affair, or even a rape. Your birth was by divine appointment. You were not only born at the right time, but the God that created this universe—the One who said, "let there be light" and light came—this God created you for a divine purpose.

Acts 17:26–27 tells us that God "has made from one blood every nation of men to dwell on all the face of the earth, and has determined their preappointed times and the boundaries of their dwellings, so that they should seek the Lord, in the hope that they might grope for Him and find Him." Our divine appointments in life or our seasons are linked to our purposes both chronologically and geographically.

We tend to get hung up on two words in the Bible: *predestined and preappointed*. Our mind tells us that we have no decision in the course of our lives. That is far from truth, because we are not puppets God manipulates through life. The Greek word for *predestined* is *proorizo,* which is a compound of two words: *pros,* which means "in front of or before," and *horizo,* which means "boundaries of time." Another Scripture clarifies those two definitions, Romans 8:29: "For whom He foreknew, He also predestined to be conformed to the image of His Son, that He might be the firstborn among many brethren." Before you were born "in front of your time," God created you to be able to be changed into the image of His Son, Jesus Christ. That is part of our purpose—to find God, become intimate with Him, and allow Him to change us into the image of His Son.

The other word, *preappointed,* is the Greek word *prostasso,* which is a combination of two words: *pros,* which means "pertaining to," and *tasso,* meaning "assign." I believe that no matter what culture or race you were born into, God placed you there in time and space. You are not a mistake or an accident; you are a man or woman with a divine plan and purpose. This is your season, and you will never have perfect peace and satisfaction until you discover and begin to fulfill your divine purpose.

God told the prophet Jeremiah,

> Before I formed you in the womb I knew [and] approved of you [as My chosen instrument], and before you were born I separated and set you apart, consecrating you; [and] I appointed you as a prophet to the nations. Then said I, Ah, Lord God! Behold, I cannot speak, for I am only a youth. But the Lord said to me, Say not, I am only a youth; for you shall go to all to whom I shall send you, and whatever I command you, you shall speak. Be not afraid of them [their faces], for I am with you to deliver you, says the Lord. Then the Lord put forth His hand and touched my mouth. And the Lord said to me, Behold, I have put My words in your mouth. (Jeremiah 1:5–9 AMP)

God didn't create you to be a little blessing to fill up your parents' photo album. He created you for a purpose. Even before Jeremiah's father's sperm united with his mother's egg in her womb, God said He knew Jeremiah. *Knew* is the Hebrew word *yada,* which means to know by observing, thinking about, and experiencing. It means to be intimate with someone; in fact, it is such a strong sense of intimacy, Genesis 4:1 says that Adam knew (*yada*) Eve, and she conceived Cain.

God so knew (*yada*) Jeremiah in such a way that He created him with a purpose, in the very same way God knew you. David, a man who knew his purpose, wrote in Psalm 139:13–16,

> For You formed my inward parts;
> You covered me in my mother's womb.
> I will praise You, for I am fearfully and wonderfully made;
> Marvelous are Your works,

And that my soul knows very well.
My frame was not hidden from You,
When I was made in secret,
And skillfully wrought in the lowest parts of the earth.
Your eyes saw my substance, being yet unformed.
And in Your book they all were written,
The days fashioned for me.

Those with low self-esteem compare their talents and looks with someone else's, but God fearfully and wonderfully made you. He didn't miss it with you. *Yare* is the Hebrew word for *fearfully*, and it means "to stand in awe of." When your parents first saw you, they probably said, "Isn't she beautiful?" or "Just look at my boy!" They saw your future, and they "stood in awe" of their newborn. That is way God sees you, His child created with a plan and a purpose. *Palah* is the Hebrew word for "wonderfully," which means to be separate or distinguish. God didn't make your physical features or your gifting and talents like those of anyone else; that is how much care God took in planning you.

The words "substance being unformed" means having potential. Your parents, your teachers, and even your friends may see you as someone that does not have any potential, but God knew you even before anyone knew you were conceived. And in that barely formed fetus, God saw your potential, for He divinely created you for a purpose. In fact, everyone—no matter who he or she is or when and where he or she lives—was created for a purpose to fulfill a divine destiny.

Ephesians 2:1–2 talks about our "old life": "And you He made alive, who were dead in trespasses and sins, in which you once walked according to the course of this world." Paul goes on to say that "we are His workmanship, created in Christ Jesus for good works, which God prepared beforehand that we should walk in them" (v. 10) The

English word *created* is the Greek word *ktisis,* which means "the creative act in process." You are not a finished product, but you are an ongoing project. Your goal is not to remain where you are, but to keep seeking your purpose in life by becoming more intimate with Him, hearing His voice, and allowing Him to direct your paths so that you might fulfill your purpose.

We are in this creative process to do these "works" that God has prepared for us before our "season" that we "should"—not necessarily "we would"—walk in them. To walk means to occupy or be surrounded by these works. Remember, Jesus said to John, "My food is to do the will of Him who sent Me, and to finish His work "(John 4:34), and "Greater (to a higher extent) works will you do because I go to My Father" (John 14:12, my paraphrase).

In 1 John 3:8, we learn of the purpose of Jesus: "For this purpose the Son of God was manifested, that He might destroy the works of the devil." Jesus was predestined by His Father to destroy the works of Satan that kept His children enslaved to sin, sickness, and bondage. Every instance in the preceding Scriptures that the word *work* is used, it is the Greek word *ergos.* You have a work to do to fulfill your purpose and that is to do the "will of your Father God" and to do the same works Jesus did.

Ernest Hemingway, one of the most distinguished authors in modern times in regard to life, said, "I live in a vacuum that is lonely as a radio tube when the batteries are dead and there is no current to plug into." Later he took his life, feeling unfulfilled. Hemingway was not an isolated case; in fact, he was probably the norm. We all have natural gifting and talents as well as purposes, but don't confuse the two. God has given us all natural gifting and talents; Hemingway's was writing. Jeremiah 8:20 says, "The harvest is past, the summer is ended, and we are not saved!" Don't let the season of your purpose pass you by without fulfilling God's plan for your life. Hemingway used his natural gifting to the utmost, but he failed in fulfilling his purpose.

You are here on this earth for a purpose; it is up to you to position yourself so that you fulfill your purpose. If you have not discovered your purpose or reason for being, begin to seek the One who not only knows but also designed your purpose. Become acquainted with Him; learn to hear and recognize His voice by spending time with Him.

Chapter 2

POSITIONED TO PROSPER

The old saying "Be in the right spot at the right time" is often applicable. I believe that if we were all honest with ourselves, we would say that we would really like to be successful. I never met anyone that said, "When I was a child, I always wanted to grow up and become a bum, live on the streets, and beg for my existence." I think that many men have a natural desire to own property or land. Growing up as a cowboy, I often dreamed of living on a huge cattle ranch, riding horses, and working cattle. I remember reading the livestock magazines after college when I was working on a ranch making far less than minimum wage, because I wanted to cowboy for a living. I would read all the ads in the back, listing horses, cattle, and ranches for sale. At the time I had to save for an entire year to buy a new saddle, so it was beyond my wildest imaginations how anyone could afford a ranch. But I still loved to read and dream about the ranches for sale. Now there are places in the United States that consider anything over one acre a ranch, but in the Southwest, where I was born and raised, a ranch had to contain several thousand acres and often cost in the hundreds of thousands of dollars or even into the millions—far beyond a cowboy's wages.

In 1979, three years after Lou Ann and I married, I quit a good job to begin a cattle-brokering business. We had really gotten into the Word of God; we were tithing and giving offerings on all our income; and we believed God to prosper us. The business has become a memorial stone of God's faithfulness to supply our needs according to our giving, because we had absolutely no working capital to begin the new venture. We had God's favor. I was flowing in my natural gifting of buying and selling cattle, and I also was flowing in my spiritual gifting of leading a home group for college kids.

God was blessing our business to the point that Lou Ann was able to quit her job within a year and become a homemaker and eventually a mother. In 1985, we built our dream house and had two young daughters that God had produced from Lou Ann's formerly barren womb. (That's another testimony for another time.) I had stopped by the house of a friend that was in the ministry. He was out, but his wife let me in, quickly introduced me to a friend of hers that was visiting, and went back to her phone conversation.

This friend of hers and I visited in the living room about many different things. Then suddenly she got up and asked if she could pray for me. Of course I said yes. She began to pray for my family, my business, and me and then she began to pray in the Spirit. After praying for several minutes in the Spirit, she stopped and began to prophesy, saying, "All the land belongs to the Lord and He is beginning to shift it out of the hands of those that did not honor Him and His Word and put it into the hands of those whose hearts are for Him." She went on to say that God was going to give me a ranch, but could not say how.

I left there that night, excited about telling Lou Ann and feeling that something was birthed inside of me. We began to pray about this ranch, but our natural minds couldn't comprehend it, since we did not have enough money to buy one; nor did we have any relatives that owned a ranch we might inherit.

Northeastern New Mexico is some of the finest ranching country anywhere, and that was exactly where I wanted a ranch. Many times I would be there, stop my car, get out, and lie on the ground, praying, probably looking ridiculous to passing motorists. After several years we had acquired sufficient income to begin looking for a ranch to purchase. In 1992, the owner of a ranch that we had been leasing since 1979 asked if I wanted to buy it. To shorten the story up, we bought the ranch. At the closing, I asked God, "How did you give us this ranch?" He began to show me where it wasn't costing me anything, because of the tax breaks we would get from all the depreciation and that He had blessed my business to the point that I was able to make a substantial down payment.

I said to the Lord, "This sounds good, but how did You really give it to me?" The Lord asked me what my annual payment was, and that's when I realized it was nearly half of what I was paying for my lease, and on my lease I had possession only six months out of the year.

Finally, Lou Ann asked the former owner why he sold the ranch, since he had lived there most of his life. He replied, "We just always wanted Ty to have this ranch." I might add that we purchased it in 1992 for about $275,000, and in 2012 it was worth $2.5 million. God has a pretty impressive way of multiplying and bringing increase into our lives as we sow seeds into His kingdom.

Everything that Lou Ann and I have financially has been the result of positioning our lives according to biblical truths and remaining in position, even when times got tough. I shared all of this with you so you can grab the vision that God desires to prosper you far beyond your wildest imaginations, but first He must get you into position.

Genesis 1:26–28 says,

> God said, "Let Us make man in Our image, according
> to Our likeness; let them have dominion over the fish of
> the sea, over the birds of the air, and over the cattle, over
> all the earth and over every creeping thing that creeps on
> the earth." So God created man in His own image; in
> the image of God He created him; male and female He
> created them. Then God blessed them, and God said to
> them, "Be fruitful and multiply; fill the earth and subdue
> it; have dominion over the fish of the sea, over the birds
> of the air, and over every living thing that moves on
> the earth." When God formed man, breathed into man
> and man became a living being. The very next thing
> God did was He blessed him, by blessing man He (God)
> empowered or gave him the capacity to prosper.

Proverbs 10:22 says, "The blessing of the Lord makes one rich." The
word *rich* does not refer to spiritual riches, but it is the Hebrew word
ashar, which means "to increase in goods and accumulate wealth."

The next thing God spoke was to "be fruitful and multiply." *Fruitful*
does not literally mean to be "full of fruit" or "act fruity," but it is
from the word *peri,* which means rewards, riches, and wealth—and
not only riches, but *full* of riches. *Multiply* means simply "increase."
But, sadly, most people today decrease.

Now look at Genesis 2:8: "The Lord God planted a garden eastward
in Eden, and there He put the man whom He had formed." I don't
know about you, but things that aren't important to me I'm likely
just to drop anywhere, but if something is important, I carefully put
it somewhere. God didn't form Adam and then drop him onto planet
Earth. He imparted everything that this man needed into him with
faith-filled words that gave him the power to prosper in what God

intended (Isaiah 55:10). And then He put Adam in a garden that He had planted for him. Did you get the picture? Everything that Adam needed, God had provided, not by planting when Adam arrived in the garden, but planted the garden first and then putting Adam there.

Friend, everything that you have need of in this life—whether it be weapons to fight the giants you face, equipment to survive the storms, or provision to live on—God has already planted for you. Second Peter 1:2–4 says, "Grace and peace be multiplied to you in the knowledge of God and of Jesus our Lord, as His divine power has given to us all things that pertain to life and godliness, through the knowledge of Him who called us by glory and virtue, by which have been given to us exceedingly great and precious promises, that through these you may be partakers of the divine nature." All that you have need of, God has already planted for you where He put you.

You begin to harvest what He has given you by placing yourself in and under His Word, so that you have knowledge of Him. That word *knowledge* is not about what man can teach you, but refers to knowing thoroughly the character of one by spending time with and becoming intimate with to the point that you know their desires. That is why when Jesus spoke about giving you your desires, it was conditional; it requires you to abide in Him and His words to abide in you. Abiding in the Word and in Him is getting yourself in position to prosper. (John 15:7)

Before we begin to learn about positioning ourselves to prosper, let me give you my definition of what prosperity is and what it's not. Prosperity does not mean that you have four Lexus vehicles, a six-thousand-square-foot house, and a seven-figure bank account. Prosperity is not limited to you having these things. It doesn't matter to God how much He can get to you, if He can get it through you. Money is not evil; it is the love of money that is evil (1 Timothy 6:10).

My definition of prosperity is found in 2 Corinthians 9:8: "God is able to make all grace abound toward you, that you, always having all sufficiency in all things, may have an abundance for every good work." Prosperity is having sufficiency in all areas of your life. Your basic needs are probably food, shelter, clothing, and transportation. *Sufficiency* simply means having enough to meet these basic needs, but prosperity means having an "abundance for every good work." This does not mean a new bass boat or new sixty-inch plasma TV. It means when you see a good work, you can give toward accomplishing that work.

Jesus said that He came to do the "work" His Father sent Him to do; therefore, a good work would be anything that expands and builds the Kingdom of God. When God told Joshua that if he would obey, observe, and meditate on the Word of God, then he would be prosperous, and successful (Joshua 1:8). The word *success* has many meanings, including to be prudent, to act wisely, to give attention to, to ponder, and to prosper. Many Christians may be tithers and live righteous lives yet never live in sufficiency because they don't make wise decisions or ponder their spending. They got a credit card in the mail, and they think that must be God telling them to buy something. That is absurd. We are to be wise stewards of our money and live within our budgets. God's plan is not spending more than your budget, but allowing Him to increase your finances; then you can increase your budget wisely.

Often the Old Testament word for prosper is the Hebrew word *tsalach,* which means "to have a successful journey; to be profitable." Doesn't that line up with what God spoke into man's life at creation? He blessed him and told him to be fruitful and multiply (or increase) and to have dominion over everything. God not only desires the same for you, but He has also made provision for you—if you will get into position and stay there.

15

Every promise of God has a condition attached to it. As the saying goes, it takes an action on your part to bring a reaction on God's part. Look at Joshua 1: 7–8:

> Only be strong and very courageous, that you may observe to do according to all the law which Moses My servant commanded you; do not turn from it to the right hand or to the left, that you may prosper wherever you go. This Book of the Law shall not depart from your mouth, but you shall meditate in it day and night, that you may observe to do according to all that is written in it. For then you will make your way prosperous, and then you will have good success.

God said that if we want to prosper and be successful, it takes some actions on our part. We not only have to observe (by looking into) the Word; we also have to keep the Word in our minds and hearts and do what the Word says. Let me ask you, "Is tithing in the Word of God? Are we required to tithe?" A tithe according to the Word of God is 10 percent of our increase; that is not based on your net, but your gross. Tithing is not about whether you want to believe in it or something you do just when you go to church.

Tithing is all about ownership. The first 10 percent of your gross is not yours; the Bible says that it belongs to God and that it is holy. Taking something that was holy and consecrated to the Lord got Achan into trouble. He didn't take something out of Ai that belonged to the Devil; he took what belonged to God and put it with his stuff (Joshua 6:17–19; 7:11). The leaders of Isreal found what belonged to God in Achan's tent (Joshua 7:22). Achan didn't take a Babylonian garment; he took what belonged to God, which brought the curse into their lives.

Does that remind you of Malachi 3:8? "Will a man rob God? Yet you have robbed Me! But you say, 'In what way have we robbed You?' In tithes and offerings." Maybe you have not gotten into position to receive God's favor and prosperity because you have kept part or all of God's stuff and hidden it in your living room or parked it in your garage. You might say, "Well, I am redeemed from the curse" (Galatians 3:13–14). Yes, you have been, but you can get right back under by sinning and stealing from God.

Tithing is God's plan to position you so that He can open up the windows of heaven and pour out such a blessing that you won't have enough room to receive it, rebuking the devourer (the curse) from your life (Malachi 3:10–11, my paraphrase). Positioning by tithing and giving is not about when we have a financial need, but about a lifestyle of obedience in the area of ownership.

Positioning for prosperity is not only about tithing and giving; we remain in position by how we tithe and give. We talked earlier in this chapter about the definition of prosperity in 2 Corinthians 9:8: "And God is able to make all grace abound toward you, that you always having all sufficiency in all things, may have an abundance for every good work." Now, that is the reaction on God's part; let's look at the action on our part.

Second Corinthians 9:7 says, "Let each one [give] as he has made up his own mind and purposed in his heart, not reluctantly or sorrowfully or under compulsion, for God loves (He takes pleasure in, prizes above other things, and is unwilling to abandon or to do without) a cheerful (joyous, "prompt to do it") giver [whose heart is in his giving]" (AMP). God is never going to force you into position. He wants you to get there out of a desire to be obedient because you love Him and wish to please Him. Cheerful giving comes from having faith that your chosen action brings forth what you desire. Let me give you a simple example. Have you ever seen a farmer plant a

17

field of corn and then get off his tractor and begin to complain about using up his seed? Or have you seen a farmer get off his tractor and lie down on his field, sobbing uncontrollably that he won't see those seeds again? No, he planted by faith, and he is expecting a huge harvest in a few months.

Once you've gotten into position with giving back to God what belongs to Him (the tithe), then you have to maintain your position. The farmer in the preceding paragraph planted his seed, but many times he will face adversity before he sees his harvest. It may be a drought that requires some water; it may be the soil lacks nutrition, so he must fertilize; or it may be insects or disease threatening his crop and he has to spray. Regardless, he cannot neglect his crop; he must continue to maintain it.

We operate the same way as we give tithes and offerings. Galatians 6:9 says, "Let us not grow weary while doing good, for in due season we shall reap if we do not lose heart." If we are going to bring forth a harvest, we must keep on staying in position by sowing for a continual harvest. We must not give up, but keep believing. When it is time, God will bring in our harvest.

The next thing about remaining in position to walk in God's favor, success, and prosperity is keeping in position with Him. We cannot expect God to bless our lives if we continue to sin when God reveals that what we are doing is sin. Proverbs 28:13 says, "He who covers his sins will not prosper." Covering your sins is simply concealing them. We know that we can hide nothing from God; concealed sin is sin that has not been dealt with by confessing to God that it is sin, asking Him to forgive you, and repenting—that is, not repeating that sin.

Second Corinthians 5:21 says, "He (God) made Him (Jesus) who knew no sin, to be sin for us, that we might become the righteousness of God in Him." Righteousness is a position; we are righteous when standing in rightful relationship with God. But righteousness must be maintained by choosing not to sin, quickly confessing when we do sin, and asking God to forgive us. Grace and mercy do not give us the freedom to sin and are not "get out of sin free" cards. We maintain our position to prosper by staying in right relationship with God.

Paul's prayer in 3 John 1:2 is not just for Gaius; it is also our Father's will for our lives: "Beloved, I pray that you may prosper in all things and be in health, just as your soul prospers." To prosper or be successful in *all things*, you must get the revelation that it is God's will as His child for you to prosper. Knowing that it is His will is part of our being in position for Him to prosper us, for He is the one who brings success to our lives. As Deuteronomy 8:18 says, "But remember the LORD your God, for it is he who gives you the ability to produce wealth, and so confirms his covenant, which he swore to your forefathers, as it is today" (NIV).

Chapter 3

POSITIONED WITH RESPONSIBILITIES

My youngest daughter, Brandi, was and still is a "critter lover." We first learned this about her when she was still a toddler. She would catch earthworms while watching her mother work in the flowerbeds. She would hold these wiggly little worms for hours, often bringing them into the house to observe.

When she was around three years old she caught a "fuzzy" caterpillar. All day long she played with him, even holding him under her nose like a mustache. That night Lou Ann and I went out for dinner and left a baby-sitter in charge of Brandi and her big sister, Brooke. Brandi decided to give her new fuzzy wuzzy a bath, so she climbed on her little stool in front of the sink. When she turned the faucet on, the little caterpillar was suddenly washed out of her hand and down the drain.

Brandi immediately started screaming and crying at the top of her lungs. The baby-sitter rushed to see what had happened. Brandi sobbingly told her the account, so the sitter tried to appease her by saying, "It's okay. The caterpillar just went to heaven." Brandi quickly looked down the drain and asked, "You mean that is where heaven is?"

This was just the beginning of the critters Brandi brought into our lives. There were small birds that fell from their nests, baby rabbits found in the yard, plus snakes, frogs, and lizards. One time we were visiting some friends and Brandi caught some giant snails in the bushes. Well, needless to say, she had to take some home with her. In a few months, all our neighbors were amazed at all the snails that had invaded our neighborhood and had begun to destroy their plants and even crawled on their windows, leaving behind trails of gooey stuff that had to be scrubbed off.

We went from all the free catch-as-you-can creatures to cats and dogs; we always had some kind of animal living in the house. Brandi always liked the unusual, so when she spotted a weird-looking lizard in the pet store called a fire-bellied newt, she had to have him. We decided it would be a good time to teach her some responsibility. If she would agree to take care of him and clean the terrarium that already housed a hermit crab named Hermie, then we would buy Newt for her.

All started well—for a few weeks. But then Hermie escaped, and we found it in the living room about a month later. When the newness of Newt wore off, Brandi began to get lax in her responsibilities of taking care of her in-house zoo. Her responsibilities were to feed and put out fresh water daily. Also the terrarium had to be emptied weekly, the glass walls scrubbed, and the rocks and fake trees washed so no bacteria would build up and smell.

I walked in her room one day and was overcome by the fumes from a slimy lizard that had lost its tail and looked malnourished, so I gave her the alternative for not taking care of her pets. Hermie and Newt were released back into the wild of her mother's flowerbeds.

A lot of people enter God's kingdom just as Brandi's entered the world of animal caretaking. They are excited that they are saved, eager to be in the house of God, but after the new wears off, they don't want any of the responsibility that comes with kingdom living. Ephesians 2:10 says, "We are God's [own] handiwork (His workmanship), recreated in Christ Jesus, [born anew] that we may do those good works which God predestined (planned beforehand) for us [taking paths which He prepared ahead of time], that we should walk in them [living the good life which He prearranged and made ready for us to live]" (AMP).

Even before God created the earth and hung the moon and stars in heaven, even before He formed Adam from the dust of the earth and breathed life into him, God had a plan for Adam. Before the foundations of this earth were laid, God had a destiny for the man He would place on this earth. God designed humankind to live on this earth and not fail, yet Adam failed.

We've all known someone that had every opportunity to become a great success in life, only to waste them because they refused to be responsible for what had been given to them. The prodigal son in the New Testament parable was given his entire inheritance before his father died. He could have invested wisely and become very wealthy, but the Bible said he wasted his fortune on prodigal living. But then one day he realized he was in a pigpen eating what the pigs had dropped or refused to eat.

I had a friend in high school who was a natural athlete. He made the varsity football squad as a freshman and quickly became the star. He ran track and at one time held the state record for the one-hundred-yard dash. All through his sophomore and junior years, he broke records in both football and track. Coaches from major universities began to visit our hometown in hopes of signing him to play college football. While most of the rest of the team worked hard, trained hard, and kept in shape, this young athlete did the opposite. He drank, smoked, and stayed out almost every night. Finally in his senior year, which should have been his springboard into the college ranks, he was kicked off the team for failing to obey the rules.

I've known guys that have had the greatest creative minds. They excelled in school and should have ended up as CEOs of major companies, but they ended up as failures simply because they did not have a good work ethic. I've seen preachers that are so anointed and gifted by God that they should have become leaders of great churches and ministries. But because they refused to be responsible for their lives and fell into sin, they are now no longer in the ministry.

Psalm 139 reveals not only how much God knows about us, but also that, even before we were dreamt of by our parents, God put into our future the ability to be what and who He created us to be. Psalms 139:1–3 says, "O Lord, You have searched me and known me. You know my sitting down and my rising up; You understand my thought afar off. You comprehend my path and my lying down, And are acquainted with all my ways." Now look carefully at Psalm 139:13–16:

> For You formed my inward parts;
> You covered me in my mother's womb.
> I will praise You, for I am fearfully and wonderfully made;
> Marvelous are Your works.
> And that my soul knows very well.
> My frame was not hidden from You,
> When I was made in secret,
> And skillfully wrought in the lowest parts of the earth.

Now look at verse 16: "Your eyes saw my substance, being yet unformed. / And in Your book they all were written, / The days fashioned for me, / When as yet there were none of them."

Way before anyone ever thought about you being born, God looked at you, and He saw your substance. In other words, God saw what no one else has ever seen about you: He saw potential. One of the definitions of substance is "power"; you may feel powerless or think you have no potential, but God sees you as you really are: someone that has potential to succeed. The psalmist goes on to say that even before our birth, God, like a potter, shaped out our season here on this earth—this season we call life.

God didn't drop us into this season without the assets and equipment necessary to be all that He created us to be. Second Peter 1:3–4 says, "His divine power has given to us all things that pertain to life and godliness, through the knowledge of Him who called us by glory and virtue, by which have been given to us exceedingly great and precious promises, that through these you may be partakers of the divine nature." He gives us everything that you and I need not only to survive in this life, but also to be successful. God has given this to us through an impartation of His power into our lives and through His promises in His Word, the Bible.

Before God formed Adam, He planted a garden. In this place called a garden, God put everything that Adam needed to fulfill all that God had created him to be. The word *plant* means "to establish." In other words, God established the garden where He put Adam. And when God put Adam there, He also gave Adam responsibility over the garden. Possession often involves responsibility and accountability.

Remember the first time you got the keys to the car for your first date without a chaperone? You were all excited because you were going to a school dance in the gymnasium and afterward you were dropping by the Dairy Queen for a coke. In the past Mom or Dad had taken you and your date to the movies, picked you and your date up after the movie was over, then drove your date home. Now you'd passed your driver's license test, and inside your billfold was a cherished piece of paper that said, "Temporary Driver's License."

Now you are at the door, and your Dad is dangling the keys in front of you and is giving all the rules of responsibility for the privilege of using the car. You must drive carefully, observing all traffic rules and speed limits. No drinking or eating in the car either. And finally, before he hands you the keys, he says in a very sharp tone, "You better bring this car back in the same condition that you took it."

As soon as you put the key in the ignition, the car becomes your responsibility. Adam heard very similar words from God: "I have planted this garden for you, and everything that you need in life is in this garden … but you must tend it and keep it." God does the very same thing with you and me when He puts us into the kingdom through salvation. He has "given us an abundant life" (John 10:10), and He has given us all things that pertain to life and godly living (2 Peter 1:3). But He has also given us responsibilities.

Genesis 2:15 says, "Then the Lord God took the man and put him in the garden of Eden to tend and keep it." The word *tend* in the Hebrew is *abad,* which means "to serve, cultivate, enslave, work." Some translations replace *tend* with the words *dress* or *till.* Let's look back to Genesis 2:4–6: "This is the history of the heavens and the earth when they were created, in the day that the Lord God made the earth and the heavens, before any plant of the field was in the earth and before any herb of the field had grown. For the Lord God had not caused it to rain on the earth, and there was no man to till the ground; but a mist went up from the earth and watered the whole face of the ground." This garden had everything needed to produce a harvest: seeds were in the ground, capable of reproducing, and the soil was sub-irrigated for moisture. All it needed was someone responsible for taking care of it, so God put man there to tend it.

Meryl Kanny calls himself a simple man. Kanny has a mechanics shop in his garage in Durban, South Africa. He is the son of a sharecropper that learned the trade of working on cars as a young man. He worked his way up in the local dealerships and became well-known for his knowledge and abilities to repair automobiles. Kanny, an Indian, was raised in a Christian home and has served the Lord most of his life.

When the opportunity came for Kanny to go on a missionary trip to Mozambique, he eagerly went. There God spoke to him to build churches in places that had not had a church in over four hundred years. On returning to Durban, Kanny was offered promotions that would limit his missionary trips, so after prayer with his wife, Nancy, they decided to set up a shop in their garage at home. Kanny's reputation for honesty and providing good work has spread throughout the Durban area.

Kanny and his son, Dean, book cars each day for repair. To fulfill his responsibility—that is, to tend his garden—Kanny withholds 20 percent from each job to put into mission work. This is in addition to his tithe to his local church. Once a month Kanny hooks up a cargo trailer loaded with supplies of food, clothing, and candy to his Land Rover and heads out on a twelve-hour drive to Catembe, Mozambique. In the area around Catembe, Kanny, his family, and others haul in building materials and build churches. In fact, many of Kanny's customers have gotten involved and been on these missionary trips with him.

Brother Kanny is an example of someone tending where God has placed him. When we stand before God it won't make any difference what titles we held, how much we accumulated, or how many extracurricular activities we were involved in. What will matter is whether we tended and worked where God planted us. Did we expand the kingdom of God?

In John 15:1–8 Jesus talks about branches that did not bear any fruit. He says that those unfruitful branches will be cut off and burned because they were unfruitful. The Christian church today in America is decreasing while other religions are increasing at a rapid pace, because Christians are failing to tend the places where God has put them. We've become complacent about our responsibilities and uncommitted in our calling to evangelize the world.

God also told Adam to "keep" the garden where He put him. The Hebrew word for "to keep" is *shamar,* which means "to keep, tend, watch over, retain." When God formed Adam and put him into position in the garden, He knew there was an enemy out there that would try to displace and destroy the man. So God charged Adam to watch over and guard where He put him. When Jesus died on the cross, He defeated and stripped the enemy called Satan of all power. Now Satan only goes about like a roaring lion, seeking whom he can devour. The only way he can cause any damage is through an opening. A door has to be opened, a line of defense let down, or a guard not in position before Satan can enter into one's garden.

Satan enters through doors of deception. When we are under deception, we believe that the truth is not really the truth. Instead of admitting that we've been deceived, we try to justify our actions. We try to convince ourselves that it must be okay, because everyone else is doing it. We go ahead and do it because the last time we did it, God didn't strike us down with a lightning bolt, so it must be okay with Him. If Eve had guarded the truth, she would have never eaten the proverbial apple. The Word of God and only the Word of God should be our standard of what the truth is and what is okay and what is not okay.

We also have to guard against becoming desensitized. Recently I was in our mall with a friend who was shopping for clothes. He went into a chain store that is very popular with young people. The music inside the store was very loud, so I walked out into the mall to make a few phone calls. After completing my calls, I went back inside to a store, which was filled with moms shopping with their daughters and teenagers looking at the newest fashions. The music was blaring throughout the store, and all of a sudden I heard the F-word in the lyrics. As I listened more closely, it seemed liked the F-word was nearly every other word.

At first I was shocked at what I was hearing. In fact, I kept listening, thinking I wasn't hearing what I thought I was hearing, because everyone else was acting like it was okay. I ran to the manager and asked, "Do you hear the words in this song?"

He replied, "Yeah, like so what?"

"Why do you play that kind of filth in your store?" I asked.

"All our music is programmed through our corporate offices, so what you hear here, you will hear in our other stores."

There are scenes on the TV's in our living rooms that ten years ago you could only view in X-rated peep houses. Nearly all sitcoms depict and endorse homosexuality as an alternative lifestyle. Cartoons like *The Simpsons* encourage our children to rebel against parental authority. Video games encourage our children that taking lives, stealing, and having a prostitute are normal, so they play their games out in schools across America, and we are shocked. Malls sell T-shirts with explicit sexual phrases to preteens, our kids hang demonic posters in their rooms. The music industry is selling filth to our kids, and we think nothing of it. When a boxer drops his guard, his opponent usually knocks him out.

When you made Jesus Christ Lord of your life, He gave you some responsibilities. He placed you into a field, or a realm of influence.

The more responsible you become in your field of influence, the more area of influence God will give you. In our initial field, we need to become responsible over our own lives. Responsibility is making good choices and good decisions. We are to guard what tries to come into our lives that will bring destruction and separation from God. Bad influences through friendships, watching, listening to, or reading the wrong kinds of things can pollute our fields, which will cause our lives to be unproductive. God has given us the responsibility of guarding our homes, our families, and our destiny. Remember, as you learn to be responsible with what God has given you, He will entrust more to you.

Chapter 4

POSITIONED FOR YOUR MIRACLE

Lou Ann and I were returning to Austin, Texas, after going to a steer roping in San Angelo, Texas. Somewhere along that narrow two-lane highway, I got up the courage to propose marriage to her, knowing that if she said no, she probably wouldn't bail out of a pickup going seventy miles an hour. I couldn't have been more surprised with her response. A yes or no answer did not come out of her mouth but instead, there was this reply: "I need to tell you something before I answer your question."

She began to recount to me that during her early teens, she had experienced recurring female problems for which she received gynecological treatment from doctors for several years. At the age of eighteen, Lou Ann's doctors gave her the report that would hauntingly play over and over in her mind: "There isn't anything else that can be done for you. You will never be able to bear a child." Through the next several years, doctor after doctor confirmed the diagnosis.

When Lou Ann was twenty-four and I was twenty-nine, we were introduced to each other in Austin by a mutual friend. I had a beautiful six-year-old daughter, Stephanie. I had been saved two years and was really into the Word of God. When Lou Ann told me about her not being able to have children, I boldly said, "The doctor's report is not the final report, for with God all things are possible." She had received Jesus as her Lord at seventeen, and even though she went to church all those years, she had not been taught the word of faith. So she had no hope for healing until I spoke those words, which began to stir deep in her heart. Those words, which agreed with God's Word, began to play over and over in her mind to replace the report of barrenness the doctors had spoken to her all those years before.

We married in January 1976, and it was my desire to get back into the cattle business. We moved to Hereford, Texas, where I went to work with a consulting veterinarian to many of the area's commercial cattle feeding yards. Lou Ann quickly got a job with a local seed company as an administrative assistant. We were enjoying life as newlyweds, and both of us were seeking a deeper walk with God.

In September of that year a miracle happened; Lou Ann became pregnant. But shortly after, she miscarried. We were saddened about the loss, but we pressed into the Word, often spending our weekends going to retreats and conferences to encourage and build our faith. During this time, Lou Ann received the baptism of the Holy Spirit, and shortly afterward I re-received the baptism of Holy Spirit. I had received it shortly after I was saved, but my pastor rebuked me for doing it, so I walked away from the gifts of the Holy Spirit for several years. When I saw the change in Lou Ann's life, a hunger arose in me.

God was good to us in Hereford; by faith we were able to buy our first home. And it was there we saw our first creative miracle. One day at Lou Ann's job, an employee came into her office for help completing health insurance forms. Tony needed help getting insurance approval for their young son, Tony Jr., who was two and a half, to have surgery. This young boy had been unable to walk since birth, so his parents took him to a doctor to find out why. They

X-rayed the young boy and found out that he had a ball, but no hip socket. They told the parents they could do an operation on him and put in an artificial socket.

After hearing the story, Lou Ann wanted to go pray for them the night before the surgery. We went to their home and shared the good news of Jesus Christ and said we believed God could heal their child. Before we prayed, we asked if they had ever had a personal relationship with Jesus Christ. The husband said yes, but his wife said she had never received Jesus as her Lord and Savior. So we prayed with her to receive Jesus. We also shared a few Scriptures with them concerning healing. After praying with them and laying hands on little Tony Jr., and seeing nothing happen with our naked eyes, we left, saying, "Just begin to thank God for healing your son."

When they checked into the hospital the next day, the doctor requested a new set of X-rays so he could make sure he had all the measurements accurate. The X-rays came back showing the boy had a complete hip socket with the ball in place. The doctor said this was impossible, so he asked for another set of X-rays, and to his astonishment he saw again a perfect hip socket. The doctor could not explain the change since the last time he had examined the child. Very bewildered, he sent them back home. A few days later, the couple stopped by our new house with young Tony, who not only walked into our home, but also ran around the den, climbing over our furniture like any normal two-and-a-half-year-old.

Well, in that same house a few months later, Lou Ann awoke from a sound sleep one night. She got up and went into our den to pray and read the Word, sensing in her spirit it was a God appointment. Speaking to her through the Word, God promised her children from her womb that had been diagnosed as barren. The Scripture God gave her was Psalms 113:9: "He maketh the barren woman to keep house, and to be a joyful mother of children. Praise ye the Lord" (KJV).

As soon as I opened my eyes in the morning, she excitedly declared that God had given her a *rhema* word that she would be able to bear children. Where *logos* refers to the written word: *rhema* is the spoken word or utterd word. Often it is the word spoken inwardly in us by the Holy Spirit or an inner revelation. By faith, we began to buy baby furnishings and pick out names. We moved to Canyon, Texas, in 1978, where I started a new job buying cattle for a local feed yard. We told our friends and family that by faith Lou Ann was going to have a baby. They thought we had gone off the deep end. We felt a little like Abraham and Sarah, declaring something that all the reports said was impossible.

Shortly afterward, Lou Ann became pregnant for the second time, and we were exhilarated at the good news and began to praise God. But it wasn't long until Lou Ann miscarried again. This did not deter our faith, so we kept believing that God had (notice the past tense *had)* made the barren woman the mother of children. In September 1980, Lou Ann again got pregnant and carried this child three months before miscarrying for the third time.

Our friends, family and our pastors rallied around us, consoling us, but also telling us that it might not be God's will for Lou Ann to bear children. They encouraged us to adopt and even made some contacts for us. But we never had a peace about adopting. We both knew it was God's will for women to bear children, and we knew the blessings of the womb recorded in the Word. We knew Lou Ann did indeed hear from God and that He is faithful to perform His Word.

In the fall of 1981 we found out again that Lou Ann was pregnant. This time she experienced a normal pregnancy and carried our miracle, Brooke Nicole, full term. She was born on May 24, 1982.

God blessed us with another miracle on February 1, 1984, when our second daughter, Brandi Paige, was born. God is *faithful!*

There was another woman that had run out of all her resources and was in desperate need of a miracle. Mark 5:25–34 tells the account of that woman.

> Now a certain woman had a flow of blood for twelve years, and had suffered many things from many physicians. She had spent all that she had and was no better, but rather grew worse. When she heard about Jesus, she came behind Him in the crowd and touched His garment. For she said, "If only I may touch His clothes, I shall be made well." Immediately the fountain of her blood was dried up, and she felt in her body that she was healed of the affliction. And Jesus, immediately knowing in Himself that power had gone out of Him, turned around in the crowd, and said, "Who touched My clothes?" But His disciples said to Him, "You see the multitude thronging You, and You say, 'Who touched Me? And He looked around to see her who had done this thing. But the woman, fearing and trembling, knowing what had happened to her, came and fell down before Him and told Him the whole truth. And He said to her, "Daughter, your faith has made you well. Go in peace, and be healed of your affliction".

Manifest means to bring into existence what does not exist or is hidden. Second Peter 1:3–4 says, "His divine power has given to us all things that pertain to life and godliness, through the knowledge of Him who called us by glory and virtue, by which have been given to us exceedingly great and precious promises, that through these you may be partakers of the divine nature." God has given us all we need in this life through our redemption on the cross. He healed us at the same moment. He paid for our sins at the same moment, but we must position ourselves for the manifestation.

Manifestations Follow Preparations

2 Chronicles 16:9 says, "For the eyes of the Lord run to and fro throughout the whole earth, to show [manifest] Himself strong on behalf of those whose heart is loyal to Him." God is anxious to meet with you and reveal His power and majesty in your life. But it takes some preparation on your part for a manifestation of God's power. Preparation for what we are expecting is an action of our faith. We prepared for the birth of our children by confessing those things that do not exist as though they did exist (Romans 4:17). We bought baby clothes, decorated a nursery, and even picked out names. It takes an action on your part to bring a reaction on God's part.

You cannot get saved by just wanting to be saved. You must believe in your heart that Jesus is the Son of God who died and gave His life for you. You must ask Him to forgive you of your sins, and then you must confess with your mouth the Lord Jesus Christ, and then you will be saved. (Romans 10:8-10) And to walk in God's provision of prosperity, you must do what? Tithe. Jesus said, "Whatever you desire, ask, and it will given unto you." Whatever you have need of, begin to make *preparation to meet the King.*

An Impartation Produces a Revelation

First Corinthians 2:9–10 says, "Eye has not seen, nor ear heard, nor have entered into the heart of man, the things which God has prepared for those who love Him, but God has revealed them to us through His Spirit." Jesus came that you might have not only eternal life, but also life that is more than ordinary, extravagant, overflowing, and abundant here on this earth. It will take an unveiling of what God has already prepared for you, and the only way it can be revealed is through His Spirit. Hebrews 4:12 says, "The Word that God speaks is alive and full of power [making it active, operative, energizing, and effective]" (AMP). As you position yourself under the Word of God, it (the Word) will begin to unveil those things that God has prepared for you. Romans 10:17 says that "faith comes by hearing, and hearing by the word of God."

Hearing is the conduit through which faith comes; it comes through the rhema spoken Word of God. As you listen to and read the Word of God, it—being *alive*—will speak to that inner part of you. If that word is received and embraced it will produce faith. When the Word is *imparted* and *caught* it will produce a revelation of "things hoped for."

When the angel appeared to Mary, he began to tell her what God had spoken to him concerning her. He said that she would conceive a son and call His name Jesus. She said, "How can this be, since I've never been intimate with a man?" The angel *imparted* words from God that had the ability to produce *faith* and *revelation*, if Mary received them. He said, "For with God nothing will be impossible" (Luke 1:37). In the original Greek this is translated "Nothing shall be impossible with God nothing." That last nothing in the Greek is the phrase *pan rhema,* which mean "All words of God are possible." When Mary heard these words, she said, "Let it be unto me according to your words."

Before you can perceive a revelation of God's Word, you must position yourself by receiving and accepting the Word. Lou Ann had been studying and meditating on God's Word. She had read Psalm 113:9 many times, but during her sleep that night she was roused by the Spirit of God, who spoke it into her inner being. Immediately she knew that she had heard from God. After that *impartation* of the

Word, she got a revelation of becoming pregnant and birthing a child, her desire.

A Revelation Produces an Expectation

When I received the prophetic word about God blessing us with a ranch, as mentioned in a previous chapter, it was as if I had gotten pregnant with a ranch. I begin to visualize a ranch and our family riding horses and working cattle. Each day brought greater expectation of having that ranch.

Hebrews 11:1 says, "Now faith is the substance of things hoped for, the evidence of things not seen." For us to have an expectation, we must have hope. Hope is confidence that what we desire will happen. Hope is an inner image or assurance of something desired. Hope sees what we desire; hopelessness sees what we dread. Hoping is not faith, but before faith can operate we must have hope or an expectation of something desired. As long as my *expectation* is based on the Word of God, I can expect a *manifestation*. This is faith in operation.

Before Jesus returned to heaven, He told the disciples of an event that was going to happen:

> "Behold, I send the Promise of My Father upon you; but tarry in the city of Jerusalem until you are endued with power from on high." And He led them out as far as Bethany, and He lifted up His hands and blessed them. Now it came to pass, while He blessed them, that He was parted from them and carried up into heaven. And they worshiped Him, and returned to Jerusalem with great joy and were continually in the temple praising and blessing God. (Luke 24:49–52)

The disciples gathered in an upper room, praying and expecting God to reveal Himself to them. How, they did not know. Each morning they arose *expecting* the promise, and finally one day that room was filled with His presence in the form of "flaming tongues," baptizing each of them with the Holy Ghost and with power. I wonder what would have happened after a few days if they had quit expecting and gone home. Begin to believe God for something in your life, and start expecting the answers.

An Expectation Produces a Manifestation

In January 2008, Lou Ann I flew to Durban, South Africa, to minister there and also to preach at a conference in Mozambique. Our first place to minister was a conference for pastors and leaders in the bush near Catembe, Mozambique. Brother Meryl and Nancy Kanny, our hosts, picked us up at two-thirty in the morning for the thirteen-hour trip to Catembe. I knew I was the only speaker on the agenda and was to speak that day.

Road weary and dirty, we arrived at a small, white church in the middle of nowhere. Several children were playing outside, and many men were standing on the front porch, with others on the side of the building, looking in the windows. As we got out, immediately the air was filled with the most awesome worship we had ever heard. We couldn't recognize a single word, but knew they were worshiping the Most High God.

We walked around the building and crawled through a makeshift door that led to the stage. The praise team was leading worship with a group of 350 people inside a church that held 250. They sang one more song, and then they asked me to start preaching. I preached for an hour and half, took a short break, and preached another hour. I found out later that these 350-plus people had been expecting us to arrive sometime that day, so they had begun to worship. It was their expectation that kept them from going back home. They made a good decision; instead of complaining that the preacher was not there or that he might not come, they got into the presence of God by worshiping Him, which they did for four and a half hours. I'm sure we get better results worshiping God than complaining about how long we have to wait. We, in America, have become so impatient that if it doesn't happen immediately, we give up and go on to something else.

A manifestation is something brought into existence that did not exist or was hidden. Isaiah 40:31 says, "But those who wait on the Lord, / Shall renew their strength; / They shall mount up with wings like eagles, / They shall run and not be weary, / They shall walk and not faint." The word *wait* means to look for, to hope for, or to expect. We have become such a speed-oriented society. We want everything instantly. That's why we microwave, eat fast foods, and fast-forward through commercials. I believe that when we begin to "stand and believe God" for something, God is well pleased and not only hears what we've asked for but is eager to fulfill it.

I believe that *waiting* is the ultimate example of faith. The Hebrew word for "renew" means "overstep." Let me say it this way: Those that *look for, hope for,* and *expect* God will *overstep* their strength. It means that they will go beyond their natural capabilities. When you begin to *expect* God to give you a miracle, your miracle is just around the corner.

Chapter 5

Positioned For a "God Meeting"

It was a Wednesday evening, and I was running late for an appointment with a family whose grandmother was in her last stages of life. I was running late when I left my house, knowing I had very little time to get there and be at church by six-thirty for prayer. Their home was in a rural subdivision that I was vaguely familiar with, having been to their home a few years back to pray for one of the family members.

I realized after getting into the neighborhood that I had left the address and phone number at the church. I thought, *No problem. I'll just call and get someone to go into my office and find the note with the address and phone number on it.* I called many times, but much to my dismay, no one answered. I kept driving around, hoping to recognize the house or see someone outside that could direct me. Because it was a rural subdivision, nearly every house had a BEWARE OF DOG sign, so I was hesitant to go knocking on doors.

As I drove, I prayed, "God, direct me to their house. Let someone answer at the church or let me see someone outside to direct me." All of a sudden, as I was dialing the church again, I remembered my phone had a built-in GPS with maps in it. I pulled over and typed in the family's name, and up popped their phone number and address on my screen. I then pressed directions, which caused a map to pop up with streets and two flags: one blue, indicating the intersection I was parked at, and one red, marking their house. I began heading in that direction, watching the blue flag get closer and closer until I pulled up into their driveway.

GPS is the abbreviation for *global positioning system*. GPS tools came out a few years ago, and now many cars and phones have them. They use satellites to pinpoint where you are, then locate where you desire to go. They have capability to direct you on the shortest route by using the back roads and secondary roads or to direct you by taking interstates highways as much as possible. They even have the capability to direct you around road and construction sites. They even have the capability to inform you when you are off course, and unless you follow the instructions, you will not reach your desired destination.

God is trying to get us to a meeting with Him. Proverbs 3:6 says, "In all your ways acknowledge Him, And He shall direct your paths." The Hebrew word for "acknowledge" is *yada,* which means "know." Acknowledging Him is not just asking for God's approval, but rather being so intimate with Him that you are aware of His desires. The *New Living Translation* says it this way Proverbs 3:6: "Seek his will in all you do, and he will show you which path to take." God is trying to *direct* us to our divine destinies. He will go to extremes to have a meeting with you and me.

For example, God interrupted Paul on the road to Damascus to redirect his future. He interrupted my life June 22, 1972, on a ranch in the bottom of canyon in West Texas. God will go to the bottom of hell, a seedy bar, a crack house, or an adult bookstore to direct you to a meeting with Him. He has a GPS, which I call God's positioning system, to direct you to a place in your life where He can meet with you.

His directional map is His Word. Psalms 119:133 says, "Direct my steps by Your word." His Word is meant to keep us on the route to Him, and if we listen and obey it, it will also direct us around all the detours and pitfalls of life. The signal of His GPS is through the Holy Spirit. Jesus said, "When He, the Spirit of truth, has come, He will guide you into all truth; for He will not speak on His own authority, but whatever He hears He will speak; and He will tell you things to come" (John 16:13).

God wants to get you to a meeting with Him bringing you to a place of intimacy where He can reveal His desires and plans for you. It is the place where He can share His inheritance and goodness with you and the place that He can empower you with authority. Are you ready to meet with Him?

Because of their sin and failure to worship Him, God allowed His people, Israel, to be captured by their enemies and held in bondage for over four hundred years. America has been free for over 230 years, but over the years much of our freedom has deteriorated. Unless we are willing to change our direction not only as a nation, but also as individuals we will continue to allow the enemy to place us deeper and deeper into bondage. Second Chronicles 7:14 says, "If My people who are called by My name will humble themselves, and pray and seek My face, and turn from their wicked ways, then I will hear from heaven, and will forgive their sin and heal their land." If we desire God's plan for our lives, we must seek his face by seeking those meetings with Him.

After God supernaturally delivered His people, He led them to a place and gave them very specific directions to build a place "where

He would meet with them and speak intimately with them" (Exodus 25:22, my paraphrase).

To Make That Meeting, You Must Want to Have a Breakout

After four hundred years of living like slaves, mindsets and beliefs had become embedded in the people of God. They had come to the conclusion that slavery, oppression, and lack were their lot in life. Maybe life has imprinted you with mindsets and beliefs about yourself. You've seen a pattern of failure or a pattern of generational curses or a pattern of divorce or a pattern of failure—not only in your life, but also in your family's lives. It is easy to accept defeat as part of you. I had to get to that place in my life where I was "sick and tired of being sick and tired" before I wanted a breakout. Everything in my life was messed up, and I wanted change, and it was only a breakout that could get me to a place where I had a God encounter. God is trying to break you out so He can meet with you.

Maybe you have mindsets and beliefs imbedded in you regarding not only how you see God but also how you see His Word. Even though I had no spiritual background before I got saved, it didn't take long for mindsets about the Word of God to become embedded in me. I belonged to a denominational church that didn't believe in healing, baptism of Holy Spirit, or prosperity. I quickly developed the mindset that if God wanted to heal me, He would, and if He didn't want to heal me, He wouldn't. So if I got sick, I thought, *Well, God must be trying to teach me something.* It was the same with prosperity: I thought if God wanted me to be blessed financially, He would; if not, He wouldn't.

Soon after I was saved, I received the baptism of the Holy Spirit by reading a book entitled *Power in Praise*. I told my pastor about my experience and how great it was to have the indwelling of His power and a deeper revelation of His word. He quickly told me that was from the Devil and I had better quit praying in tongues.

Several years later, after studying the Word and witnessing the power of God flowing through ordinary people like me, I began to have a hunger and passion to break out of all the religious mindsets and beliefs that held me in bondage. Religion or your denomination may have taught you that God doesn't heal today or that prosperity is not for His people. Maybe you've believed that whatever happens must be God's will for you. Maybe you've even believed that God doesn't care about you or that He has more important things to take care of besides your problems.

Colossians 2:8 warns us to "beware lest anyone cheat you through philosophy and empty deceit, according to the tradition of men, according to the basic principles of the world, and not according to Christ." Philosophy, traditions, and principles created by people are all mindsets and beliefs that not only place us in bondage, but also keep us there. It takes a God encounter to break us free.

God's people who had been working as slaves and living in very harsh and impoverished conditions for several generation began to get fed up with their lifestyle, and they cried out to a God they had never seen or met with. When you get fed up with a mediocre, ordinary, or substandard life, you are a prime candidate for a breakout. Exodus 3:7–8 says, "And the Lord said: 'I have surely seen the oppression of My people who are in Egypt, and have heard their cry because of their taskmasters, for I know their sorrows. So I have come down to deliver them out of the hand of the Egyptians, and to bring them up from that land to a good and large land, to a land flowing with milk and honey.'"

Many have an awareness of God, but awareness is not intimacy with Him. Those living under the old covenant had a relationship with

44

God through their knowledge of Him. For those of us that are under the new and better covenant, our relationship with Him is with His very presence living in us. I believe that if you desire to meet with Him, He desires to meet with you even more. Just like the children of Israel, you are ready for a breakout.

To Make That Meeting, You Must Be Willing to Cross Over

We know the accounts of how God, through signs and wonders, miraculously set His people free from bondage. Two and a half million former slaves left Egypt that day, carrying their former masters' gold, silver, and other possessions. I believe that most of those that were delivered that day never had a vision of being freed. God told Moses to tell Pharaoh, "Let my people go, so they can worship me in the wilderness" (Exodus 7:16 NLT). God's purpose for you and me is not only to give us abundant life here and eternal life in heaven, but also to bring us to a place of intimacy with Him. Worship is what brings us into His presence, where we can commune with Him.

Most of those that came out of Egypt that day probably came out because everyone else was coming out. It was the thing to do; it meant no more brick making, no more abuse, and a promise of a better lifestyle. The same thing happens today. Statistics say that less than 2 percent of people that respond to an altar call really experience a changed life. I believe that some come needing to put a Band-Aid on their problems. Others come because their friends and family responded to the altar call. Probably most of those that left Egypt that day came out following others. A true God encounter is a change that is not only obvious to those around you, but also to you. Second Corinthians 5:17 says, "Therefore, if anyone is in Christ, he is a new creation; old things have passed away; behold, all things have become new."

The children of Israel looked up and saw that the Egyptians had come to the realization that they no longer had slaves and were now pursuing them so they could subdue them again.

> And when Pharaoh drew near, the children of Israel lifted their eyes, and behold, the Egyptians marched after them. So they were very afraid, and the children of Israel cried out to the Lord. Then they said to Moses, "Because there were no graves in Egypt, have you taken us away to die in the wilderness? Why have you so dealt with us, to bring us up out of Egypt? Is this not the word that we told you in Egypt, saying, 'Let us alone that we may serve the Egyptians'? For it would have been better for us to serve the Egyptians than that we should die in the wilderness. (Exodus 14:10–12)

They had gotten to the place that they had to take the risk of going in the direction of God. If you are not continually moving toward God, you are in a very critical place. You will either give up, or the enemy will overtake you. Jesus spoke more about following Him rather than just believing in Him. Our God encounters come when we are in pursuit of Him, because we love Him, and where He is going we want to be there also.

Many Christians never get to that place of meeting with God because there never was any real commitment at the altar or commitment to keep seeking Him. Many also never make it to the meeting place with God because they keep getting drawn back to where they came from.

To Make That Meeting, You Have to Start Trusting God

Trust is a firm belief or confidence in the honesty, integrity, and reliability of another to do what he or she says. I believe that one of the greatest statements in the Bible is "Abraham believed God." What a remarkable faith Abraham displayed when a God he had never seen, never heard, and never worshiped called him out of his place of comfort to a place he had never seen.

It should be so much easier for you and me to trust God by faith than it was for Abraham. We have the written Word and testimonies; we've seen God move; and we have the Holy Spirit living inside us. In this place known as the "wilderness," the people had to rely and trust in God instead of themselves or their past resources.

The more you rely on Him, the closer you will come to Him. Trust and reliance develops a relationship of intimacy. Hebrews 11:6 says, "But without faith it is impossible to please Him, for he who comes to God must believe that He is, and that He is a rewarder of those who diligently seek Him." Let me define the phrase "diligently seek" for you. It is the Greek word *ekzeteo,* which implies having a strong desire for and to worship. If you really want a meeting with God, begin to desire that place and time with Him. Throw away all those preconceived mindsets and beliefs about worship, and begin to worship with all your heart and with the intensity of your soul. All of the sudden, you will find Him in your presence, giving audience to you.

To Make That Meeting, You Must Be Willing to Make It Happen

> Then the Lord spoke to Moses, saying: "Speak to the children of Israel, that they bring Me an offering. From

everyone who gives it willingly with his heart you shall take My offering. And this is the offering which you shall take from them: gold, silver, and bronze; blue, purple, and scarlet thread, fine linen, and goats' hair; ram skins dyed red, badger skins, and acacia wood; oil for the light, and spices for the anointing oil and for the sweet incense; onyx stones, and stones to be set in the ephod and in the breastplate. And let them make Me a sanctuary, that I may dwell among them. According to all that I show you, that is, the pattern of the tabernacle and the pattern of all its furnishings, just so you shall make it." (Exodus 25:1–9)

The Hebrew word for "let them make" is *asah*, which means "to create." God had created everything necessary for the place where He was going to meet them, but He would not build it for them. There were three things necessary to build the sanctuary other than the materials. You need the same three things in order for you to meet with Him.

1. Desire. You have to have the desire to meet with God—and not for what He can give you or what He can do for you. God is not a big wish book to give you everything you want, but He wants you to have the desires of your heart as long as they are in the boundaries of His will. He is not the emergency-room tech to fix all your problems, but He desires to do so. He just wants you to desire to meet with him, and He will add all others things to you.

2. Sacrifice. Meetings with God often come unexpectedly, but most times they come when we are willing to give up something to meet with Him. For example, often when we fast—giving up food—God miraculously shows up. At our church, Arena of Life, we have an annual New Year's Eve service. This service usually focuses on the prophetic; therefore I prepare for it differently than I do our weekly services. I have an extended time of fasting and prayer, seeking God and His voice. I ask Him to speak to me concerning my life, our church, and our nation for the coming year.

Last year during this season of prayer and fasting, I heard God say, "I have scheduled an appointment with you." Wow! God had set apart time for me. I read the Word, prayed, went to prayer time at the church that night, came home, and went to bed. Honestly I had forgotten about our meeting, even though throughout the day I was expecting Him to show up.

In the middle of the night, I woke and felt so refreshed and awake that I thought it must be time to get up. I lay there for a couple of minutes, and then I remembered His words. I thought to myself, *If it's three in the morning, this must be my appointment with God.* I went into the bathroom, looked at my cell phone, and it was 3:02. (Remember, I had been lying in bed for a couple of minutes.) I ran into my office and said, "Sorry I'm late, but I am here for my appointment." God directed me to a particular chapter in the Bible and said, "This word is for you." I began to write down all the things God was speaking to me as I read each verse. Nearly everything He promised me that night has already come to pass.

Fasting and seasons of prayer are sacrifices on our part, because we give up things we think are valuable to us, such as food and time. And when we give our sacrifices, *He shows up.*

3. An Action. An action on your part will bring a reaction on God's part. We have to believe in order to receive. We have to repent to be forgiven. We have to give in order to receive.

Chapter 6

POSITIONED TO HEAR FROM GOD

A large commercial airliner takes off from LaGuardia Airport en route to Johannesburg, South Africa. The captain banks the plane to the right after gaining altitude for the nonstop flight of eighteen hours. The giant plane is headed like an arrow to its target. A few moments after making the initial turn and putting the airplane on its course, they encounter a dense fog that cuts visibility to a few hundred feet.

Airline pilots are accustomed to flying through conditions where they have no visibility. With the aid of radios, GPS, radar, and other navigational tools, they are able to keep their plane on course without using the naked eye.

As the pilot's ability to see succumbs to the fog, he radios the control tower, where his bearings are confirmed and the plane's course is redirected to avoid a tropical storm that lies between it and the African continent. The captain and his copilot flip on the radar screen, log in their destination, put their plane on autopilot, and relax for a long flight into Johannesburg.

Two hours into the flight, they lose all radio contact; all their instruments blink several times before shorting out. They had set their autopilot on, but during electrical shortages, it also fails. Now they are thousands of miles over the Atlantic with no instruments to guide them and no radio contact to confirm their location and redirect them, if necessary. Without their radar, they do not know if they are flying away from the tropical storm or into it. In fact, they do not know if they are headed to their destination or away from it. Even after the sun comes up in a few hours, flying over water that all looks the same will only confuse them more.

Several hundred men, women, and children onboard have put their trust in them. Some are headed back to their homes after a week's business trip to the States; others are headed for the vacation of a lifetime. Their lives and hundreds of others are at stake; a wrong choice could jeopardize all of them. Just as quickly as they lost communication, their radar comes back on; the GPS beeps, indicating where they are; and with a few corrections, they are back on course, diverting a major tragedy.

Just as it was of vital importance for the pilots to know not only where they were going and exactly where they were, it is vital for you and me to know the plans that God has for us.

> "For I know the plans I have for you," says the Lord. "They are plans for good and not for disaster, to give you a future and a hope. In those days when you pray, I will listen. If you look for me wholeheartedly, you will find me. I will be found by you," says the Lord. "I will end your captivity and restore your fortunes. I will gather you out of the nations where I sent you and will bring you home again to your own land." (Jeremiah 29:11–14 NLT)

The most important thing in life is for us to find God and build a relationship with Him. The second most important thing is learning to hear and recognize His voice. Every major course direction in my life has come from hearing God's voice. My successes have come from learning to hear and to recognize God's voice.

Life is full of lurking storms and disasters, many of which could be avoided if we only knew what we were headed into. God, who being good by nature and having good plans for you and me, would desire to divert us around those things. God never leads us into a marriage that ends in a horrible divorce, leaving us scarred for life. He never guides us into an investment that will fail and drain our life savings. In fact, He never tells you anything that would harm you or cause you to fail. God knows all things. He not only knows your tomorrows, He also wants to reveal your tomorrows to you.

There are many opportunities God would like to direct us to, but in order to do this; He must be able to communicate with us. It has been said that success depends on being in the right place at the right time. God wants to communicate those right places and right times. Prayer is not just a one-way conversation of us expressing our desires and needs to God, but was meant for God to express His desires and plans to us.

In Mark 4:13–20, Jesus teaches the importance of what we do with the Word of God—that we hear to the degree of success in our lives. In verses 24 and 25, He expounds on hearing God's voice: "Consider carefully what you hear. With the measure you use, it will be measured to you—and even more. Whoever has will be given more; whoever does not have, even what he has will be taken from him" (NIV). How you handle the voice of God will determine whether you live a blessed life or a cursed life; therefore, it is important that we hear His voice.

You mean to tell me that my destiny is connected to my hearing, recognizing, and following God's voice? *Yes!* Deuteronomy 28:1–2 says, "Now it shall come to pass, *if* you diligently obey the voice of the LORD your God, to observe carefully all His commandments which I command you today, that the LORD your God will set you high above all nations of the earth. And all these blessings shall come upon you and overtake you, because you obey the voice of the LORD your God."

You mean to tell me that God's blessings are contingent on my obeying God's voice? *Yes!* God is like my personal life coach, as I hear His voice and obey His voice, He guides me into my destiny. As Proverbs 3:6 says, "In all your ways acknowledge Him, And He shall direct your paths." *Acknowledge* here means to recognize and respond to His voice. Look at this Scripture from *The Message* version: "Listen for GOD's voice in everything you do, everywhere you go; he's the one who will keep you on track" (Proverbs 3:6).

Many Christians seem to experience great difficulty in communicating with their heavenly Father, especially in the area of hearing from God. We all face decisions on a daily basis for which we need direction, wisdom, and answers. I believe that God loves us so much that He is interested in every detail of our lives, but also He loves us so much that He will never try to micromanage our lives. Sometimes we think that whatever happens was probably meant to be. This is not true, God has plans for us, but the enemy also has plans, and his plans are never good.

We ask, wanting to hear from God, but we often are frustrated, feeling that God doesn't care or we are unable to hear His voice. I remember how excited I was as a new Christian hearing God speak to me for the first time. His voice was so loud in my pickup that day, I turned to see who was riding with me, only to see an empty seat. Yet there were times that I really needed to hear from God but didn't. I prayed and strained to what seemed like no avail. I was frustrated because I felt like I *never* heard His voice. I thought *God must not care.* Other times I thought I heard His voice, yet I felt confused, not knowing if I heard His voice, the voice of the enemy, or even my own voice.

Through becoming intimate with Him, I've learned that He is constantly speaking to me; I just haven't been listening. I've learned that when I need to hear His voice, I can expect to hear His voice. I want to tell you this: God not only desires to speak to you, but also *is* speaking to you. You just have to be able to distinguish His voice in a noisy world. Let me share with you some important facts concerning hearing from God.

Fact #1: God Has You Pinpointed

Several years ago, I was in El Paso, Texas, doing some cattle business. There was a restaurant in Juarez, Mexico, that was one of my favorites, so I decided I'd go there for dinner. My hotel was only a few blocks from the international border, but I didn't want to drive my truck across because of the long lines at customs. So I opted to take a trolley across, knowing that one of its stops was across the street from the restaurant.

As I headed to the station, I heard God say, "Don't go." I knew it was God speaking, but I analyzed the situation, thinking, *I'm just going to eat and come right back.* All along the ride, I kept hearing His voice, so when the trolley stopped at the right place, I didn't get off, but continued on the route to all the restaurants and tourist stops of this border city. Finally I arrived back at my hotel and turned on the TV to hear a breaking news story. One hundred bodies had been found in an unmarked mass grave on the outskirts of Juarez. All travel back into United States had been abruptly stopped as the DEA, FBI, US Customs, and other agencies investigated the crime. If I had stayed even long enough to eat a meal, I would have been detained either until the next day or in a long security line for many hours. Even though I was several hundred miles from home, God knew where I was, I recognized His voice, and He protected me.

There are times that we feel like we are so separated, so distant from God that we cannot hear His voice. In 1 Kings 18, the prophet Elijah called down fire from heaven, executed 450 prophets, broke a three-and-a-half-year drought through effectual prayer, and then got word that the wicked Jezebel was out to kill him. Elijah holed up in a cave where the "word of the Lord came to him." Elijah may have thought he was in a place where even God couldn't find him.

Remember the pilots of the crippled airliner, who had lost all communication with the tower. The tower knew their exact location and what was going on around them. In the same way, God knows where you are and where you are headed, and He desires to direct you to your destiny. The psalmist says,

> I can never escape from your Spirit! I can never get away
> from your presence! If I go up to heaven, you are there; if
> I go down to the grave, you are there. If I ride the wings
> of the morning, if I dwell by the farthest oceans, even
> there your hand will guide me, and your strength will
> support me. I could ask the darkness to hide me and the
> light around me to become night—but even in darkness I
> cannot hide from you. (Psalm 139:7–12 NLT)

Fact #2: Anybody and Everybody Can and Will Hear God's Voice

Many believe that only a few "chosen" people can hear God's voice. One of the most frequent statements I hear as a pastor is "I just can't seem to hear from God." That can be very frustrating to someone needing an accurate answer immediately. Sometimes they feel like they can't hear, so they ask, "Pastor, I just need to hear from God. Will you help me? If He tells you something, will you tell me?"

God will often go to extremes to speak to us. Several years ago, a waitress was driving down one of Amarillo's streets, listening to the Bee Gees on her radio. All of a sudden, the singing stopped, and she heard a voice coming from her radio calling her name, saying He loved her and that He wanted her to live eternally with Him. The next Sunday, this shocked waitress made her way to our church to give her life to Jesus Christ.

When God created man, He gave man the ability to hear His voice and also the ability to communicate back to Him. In our first awareness of God, as recorded in Genesis, God spoke to Adam and Eve, and they spoke to God. I believe that their conversations in the Garden of Eden were much like our conversations with people that we are close to.

For you to fulfill your divine destiny and purpose, you must learn to hear His voice. God will go to extremes to speak to you. In fact, you don't even have to be a believer to hear the voice of God, as shown in the example above. Abraham heard from God before he was in covenant with Him, and Paul heard from God before his conversion on the road to Damascus. What you thought was a tugging on your heart at an altar call or a sense that you were missing something in your life was that "still small voice" of God bringing you into that intimate relationship with Him. Revelation 3:20 says, "Behold, I stand at the door and knock. If anyone hears My voice and opens the door, I will come in to him and dine with him, and he with Me." Times of great intimacy come from sitting at the dinner table. God wants to sit down, not only to listen to your heart, but also to convey through words His own heart.

Fact #3: Since the Beginning Satan Has Tried to Separate Man from the Voice of God and Cause Man to Follow His (Satan's) Voice

Look at Adam and Eve's encounter with Satan in the garden:

> Now the serpent was more cunning than any beast of the field which the Lord God had made. And he said to the woman, "Has God indeed said, 'You shall not eat of every tree of the garden'?" And the woman said to the serpent, "We may eat the fruit of the trees of the garden; but of the fruit of the tree which is in the midst of the garden, God has said, 'You shall not eat it, nor shall you touch it, lest you die.'" Then the serpent said to the woman, "You will not surely die. For God knows that in the day you eat of it your eyes will be opened, and you will be like God, knowing good and evil." (Genesis 3:1–5)

Did you notice that even Satan knew that God had spoken to His creation. Did you see how Satan deceived Eve; he didn't tell her to eat of the tree, but he gets her to question the voice of God. "Has God indeed said …?" If Satan can separate you from the voice of God, he will not only defeat you, but he will encourage you to follow his voice. Satan so deceived them that after they disobeyed God's voice, they became "afraid of His voice and hid" (Genesis 3:10). Satan is constantly telling us that God's Word is not true, it is not relevant, and it doesn't apply to our lives. His voice is trying to get you out of the will of your heavenly Father in order to destroy your destiny and cause you to fail.

Fact #4: There Are Many Voices but Only One Shepherd

Jesus said in John 10:1–5,

> "Most assuredly, I say to you, he who does not enter the sheepfold by the door, but climbs up some other way, the same is a thief and a robber. But he who enters by the door is the shepherd of the sheep. To him the doorkeeper opens, and the sheep hear his voice; and he calls his own sheep by name and leads them out. And when he brings out his own sheep, he goes before them; and the sheep follow him, for they know his voice. Yet they will by no means follow a stranger, but will flee from him, for they do not know the voice of strangers."

Every choice produces *something,* and behind every *choice* is a *voice.* Every decision you and I make is because we heard an inner voice. You will hear other voices; therefore you need to be able to recognize them so you don't follow them. I am very bad at remembering names, but I'm good at recognizing voices. I talk to many different people by phone daily. If we have talked in the past a few times, I recognize their voice. You will hear the voice of God, of Satan, and of people, as well as your inner voice (soul). Your life and your future depend on your ability to discern God's voice from the other voices.

Out of nowhere, another voice came out of the garden, the voice of Satan questioning the voice of God: "Did God indeed say…?" Satan will try to twist the word of God so that you will rebel against it. For you to follow the truth, it is important that you know the truth. Satan's nature is to kill, steal, and destroy your life and your destiny. The good news is he doesn't have the power or authority to do it for 1 John 3:8 says, "For this purpose the Son of God was manifested, that He might destroy the works of the devil." Satan's strategy is not to make you sin or to destroy you, for he no longer has the power to do so (Romans 6:14), but to separate you from the word (God's voice), so that you will sin and make choices that will bring disaster.

God gave Saul the command to "utterly destroy all the enemy" (1 Samuel 15), but he was swayed by peer pressure. This one disobedience robbed him not only of his destiny, but also eventually his life. Afterward, Saul said to Samuel, "I have sinned, for I have transgressed the commandment of the Lord and your words, because I feared the people and obeyed their voice" (1 Samuel 15:24). Often those that are close to us want to give us counsel that doesn't line up with God's voice. Many times they are not meaning to be harmful, but they are simply operating under their carnal nature. When Lou Ann received a word from God that she would bear children after two miscarriages, several friends and family members discouraged us from continuing to believe God for children. They advised us to use common sense, saying that it would be best to adopt a child. If we had followed their counsel, Brooke and Brandi, and our four grandchildren, would not be here.

Many destinies have been crushed because somebody talked someone into compromising a word of God. They might tell you: "Go ahead, everyone else is doing it. It won't hurt." "Marry him. He will change." "Try that venture, and you will fail." "You are not qualified for the ministry." Don't settle for second best; if God spoke it, He will fulfill it. Romans 16:17–19 tells us to "watch out for people who cause divisions and upset people's faith by teaching things contrary to what you have been taught. Stay away from them. Such people are not serving Christ our Lord; they are serving their own personal interests. By smooth talk and glowing words they deceive innocent people" (NLT).

The loudest voice you probably will hear is your own. It is your *inner voice*, which consists of your soul or your mind, your will, and your emotions. It is the voice of your flesh. (In the next chapter I will do more in-depth on this.) Our flesh tells us what we desire, what we need, what we must have, and we are so used to listening to it that we refuse to listen to other voices. Often this voice gets us into bondage, causes us to sin, and entices us into wrong decisions that cost us our future.

The voice that you follow is the voice that you trust the most and are most intimate with. Recognizing God's voice comes from being intimate with Him. Intimacy comes from spending time with Him, getting to know His character and His nature. His voice will always line up with His Word. If the voice you hear is contrary to His Word that is a red flag.

John 16:13–14 says, "When He, the Spirit of truth, has come, He will guide you into all truth; for He will not speak on His own authority, but whatever He hears He will speak; and He will tell you things to come. He will glorify Me, for He will take of what is Mine and declare it to you." You *do* have the ability to hear from God.

Let me add that *circumstances* are not necessarily God's voice. As a young Christian, I remember my pastor telling me that sometimes God has to get us on our back, referring to a calamity or a sickness in order to speak to us. God loves you and me too much to bring pain in order to speak to us; however God often will take *what was meant for evil and turn it towards our good*. I once had someone who had prayed about a certain venture that was their heart's desire. He was sure that he had heard from God to step out in faith and do this particular venture. After the venture failed miserably costing him his entire savings, the man said, "Well I guess that is God's way of telling me no." Often the enemy causes things to go wrong, not God.

FACT #5: Satan Wants You to Believe That Listening to the Voice of God Will Be Disastrous for You

Satan will try to convince you that if you listen to God, it will kill your life, kill your relationships, kill your finances, kill your future, and even kill your fun. Remember this: The Bible says that Satan is the father of all lies. Stop listening to him; it is not the truth.

Fact #6: You Can Both Hear God's Voice and Ask Him to Speak to You and to Direct You

Proverbs 3:6 says, "Listen for God's voice in everything you do, everywhere you go; he's the one who will keep you on track" (*The Message*). We need to have our ears open, always listening to God's voice. I have learned from experience that when someone comes to mind, I need to pray for them or call them. I don't know how many hundreds of times I've be driving along when someone's name pops into my mind. Often I would call and often they would say they were thinking about calling me to sell some cattle. I would be in their vicinity, and instead of making another trip of several hours, I would go right to their place to buy the cattle. This saved lots of money and fuel. Many times I would hear God say, "Sell cattle now," which I would do. And immediately the price would fall. God knows all things, and He is willing to share His inside information. Praise the Lord!

We are told to "pray without ceasing," but also to listen without ceasing. James 1:5–8 tells us,

> If any of you lacks wisdom, let him ask of God, who gives
> to all liberally and without reproach, and it will be given
> to him. But let him ask in faith, with no doubting, for
> he who doubts is like a wave of the sea driven and tossed

by the wind. For let not that man suppose that he will receive anything from the Lord; he is a double-minded man, unstable in all his ways.

There is nothing in your life that God doesn't care about, and He is anxious to give you solutions. Dr. Oral Roberts once told me that before every major decision he made, he prayed in the Spirit then waited for God to speak back to him. Psalm 37:23 says, "The Lord directs the steps of the godly. He delights in every detail of their lives" (NLT). God has a plan for your life, so how can He get you to stay in the path except through speaking to you?

Fact #7: If You Have Followed Other Voices, God Can Still Direct You Back on Course

Jesus said, "Be careful what you are hearing. The measure [of thought and study] you give [to the truth you hear] will be the measure [of virtue and knowledge] that comes back to you—and more [besides] will be given to you who hear" (Mark 4:24 AMP). If we are going to hear God speak, we must have not only a desire to hear His voice, but also a desire to spend intimate time alone with Him. Where you find Him, you will find His voice. What you give ear to will create an environment for listening.

Jesus said in Matthew 6:21, "Wherever your treasure is, there the desires of your heart will also be" (NLT). Those things that we treasure or put high value on will be what catch our ear. I am a huge Texas Tech Red Raider fan. I could be in an extremely crowded room with laughter and multiple conversations going on, and if someone on the other side of the room mentions Texas Tech, all of a sudden my focus is there. As you begin to *listen* for God's voice, even in the midst of chaos, you will hear Him, because you've developed an awareness of His voice.

Chapter 7

POSITIONED TO OVERCOME

Remember therefore how you have received and heard; hold fast and repent. Therefore if you will not watch, I will come upon you as a thief, and you will not know what hour I will come upon you. You have a few names even in Sardis who have not defiled their garments; and they shall walk with Me in white, for they are worthy. He who overcomes shall be clothed in white garments, and I will not blot out his name from the Book of Life; but I will confess his name before My Father and before His angels. "He who has an ear, let him hear what the Spirit says to the churches." (Revelation 3:3–6)

To overcome means to prevail over an opponent or to succeed in dealing with a problem or a difficulty. All of us have overcome certain things. Yours may have been something of a physical or physiological nature, such as shyness. Wes James, a friend of mine, was born with a stutter, but through prayer and training, he has overcome that. Now he is an anointed singer, songwriter, and musician; he has led worship around the world.

Some have overcome poverty to become very successful. Others have overcome addictions that were destroying their lives. There used to be an introduction to a sports program that showed a skier taking a horrible fall off a ski lift. The slogan was "the thrill of victory and the agony of defeat." When we finally overcome things in our lives, we feel victorious. Succumbing to certain weaknesses made me feel defeated, guilty, and sometimes just wanting to give up. However, when I finally overcame those tendencies, I felt the thrill of victory. Several years ago, we were in Las Vegas for the National Finals Rodeo. I realized that even though I was in the center of sin city, I was not attracted by or tempted to sin. Why? Because he who the Son sets free is free indeed. Through Jesus I had overcame those things that caused me to be defeated. I truly understood what it meant to be more than a conquer through Him (Romans 8:37).

Christianity wasn't meant to be miserable, but to many, the Christian walk is very difficult. Sadly many live defeated lives; some are bound by sins, and others fall away from their faith, returning to their old lifestyle "as a dog returns to its own vomit." (2 Peter 2:2) There is our "new nature," which desires to live right, and there is our "old nature," which keeps pulling us down. About the time that we feel like we have our "old self" conquered, it comes back to trip us up and leaves us feeling miserable, unworthy to receive anything from God, and sometimes even like giving up.

Christians often find themselves committing the same sins over and over, wanting to stop but feel powerless over sin. But the Bible teaches us that we have dominion over sin (Romans 6:14).The apostle Paul, who experienced the same battles you and I face, said, "I don't really understand myself, for I want to do what is right, but I don't do it. Instead, I do what I hate." (Romans 7:15) We desire to be free of addictions and habits, knowing that John 8:36 says, "If the Son makes you free, you shall be free indeed." We often struggle with commitment to pray and study the Word. We realize that faith will change our circumstances, but we never seem to be able to operate in it. In this chapter we will discover the root cause of our spiritual "failures" and unveil the answer to living an *overcoming life.*

To find out why we fail, we must first understand who we are.

> Then God said, "Let Us make man in Our image, according to Our likeness; let them have dominion over the fish of the sea, over the birds of the air, and over the cattle, over all the earth and over every creeping thing that creeps on the earth." So God created man in His own image; in the image of God He created him; male and female He created them. Then God blessed them, and God said to them, "Be fruitful and multiply; fill the earth and subdue it; have dominion over the fish of the sea, over the birds of the air, and over every living thing that moves on the earth". (Genesis 1:26–28)

The Hebrew word for "image" is *tselem,* which means copy or replica of someone or something. We know by observation that no one in the physical world looks like God, yet we are a copy or replica of Him. Adam was formed from the dust of the earth and his wife, Eve, was taken from one of Adam's ribs, so he could not have looked like God in the physical, because God is bigger and greater than all of His creation.

To be an image of someone not only means in the physical realm, but also in that person's nature. God intended for the human race to be an image of His nature. Jesus was God in the flesh, and in the physical realm He probably resembled other men, but in the spiritual realm, His wisdom, love, dominion, and power set Him apart from the rest of mankind. He said this when Phillip asked to see His Father: "Have I been with you so long, and yet you have not known Me, Philip? He who has seen Me has seen the Father; so how can you say, 'Show us the Father'?" (John 14:9). Jesus was simply saying that He was the image of God.

On the other hand, *likeness* means being comparable without being the original. Most products we buy are created in the image and likeness of something. They are made with molds, patterns, or jigs to produce something that has all the attributes of the original. As long as you have the mold, you can always create a replica. The good news is that we have the pattern of living the successful Christian life—patterned after the original, Jesus Christ, and empowered by the indwelling Holy Spirit.

When God formed man he "breathed" into him—that is, He imparted into man His Spirit—and man became a living being. The spirit of man was in the likeness of God, and he had all His attributes without being God. That is why the angels after creation were awed at this man they saw walking in the garden. The psalmist wrote, "What is man that You are mindful of him, and the son of [earthborn] man that You care for him? Yet You have made him but a little lower than God [or heavenly beings], and You have crowned him with glory and honor. You made him to have dominion over the works of Your hands; You have put all things under his feet" (Psalm 8:4–6 AMP).

When we have a God encounter where He comes into our lives and changes the course of our eternity, there is a dramatic inward transformation. Second Corinthians 5:17 says, "Therefore if any person is [ingrafted] in Christ (the Messiah) he is a new creation (a new creature altogether); the old [previous moral and spiritual condition] has passed away. Behold, the fresh and new has come!" (AMP). The Greek word for *old* here is *archaios,* which means "original" or "from the beginning." Before our rebirth, our nature was dead or fallen. The word *new,* on the other hand, is the Greek word *kainos,* which means "not new in time, but new as to form or quality." To be *new* is to be of a different nature. To be a new creation literally means to be brand-new from the foundation up, not a makeover or remodel. One reason some people fail is that they have a belief that they must try to live this new life simply by changing themselves through self-improvement and self-denial. Reading the Bible and going to church are great and necessary tools to living a successful Christian life, but without rebirth, they are simply self-help, which under right conditions results in spiritual failure.

Adam and Eve walked in complete authority and dominion. They were in constant fellowship with God, enjoying all their privileges, until they did the only thing that could strip them of their legal rights: they disobeyed God's commands and sinned. What caused them to sin? Many say, "Well, it was the old serpent, Satan." But it was impossible for Satan to make them sin. Remember, God gave man dominion and authority over every living thing, including Satan. It wasn't Adam and Eve's spirits, because they were created in God's image. It was not their sinful nature, because they had never known sin. They had always lived in the boundaries of God's laws— until Satan suggested going outside of them.

So, what caused them to sin? It was the very same thing that causes you and me to sin and walk back into our old nature. It was their "soulish" nature. We are like God, a triune being. We are made up of a body. This physical body of ours cannot sin; it is just flesh, bone, and blood. It will cease to be at physical death and will return to the dust of the earth. We also have a spirit that is eternal by nature. It will either live for eternity in heaven with God or live eternally in hell with Satan, all his demons, and those that have refused to follow Jesus Christ. The third part of our makeup is our soul. *Psuche* is the Hebrew word for it, from which we get the words *psyche* and *psychology*. The soul is made up of our minds, our wills, and our emotions. When we learn to control these, we are able to walk victoriously and even supernaturally. Remember that Jesus, our pattern, was all God, but

Ty Jones

He was also all man, having the desires and emotions of natural man. "For we do not have a High Priest Who is unable to understand and sympathize and have a shared feeling with our weaknesses and infirmities and liability to the assaults of temptation, but One Who has been tempted in every respect as we are, yet without sinning" (Hebrews 4:15 AMP).

Considering we were all raised in different cultures and different lifestyles, our morals tend to vary, but basically before you were born again, you operated under the influence of your soul. If you were raised in an extreme puritanical home, the morals and teachings that were instilled in you probably kept you out of such things as sexual sins and drug and alcohol use, but if you were raised in a very liberal home, you may have been more apt to get involved in sexual sins and addiction to drugs and alcohol. However, no matter how or where we were raised, looming inside all of us is the soulish nature that desires to rebel against the sovereignty of God. Romans 8:5–8 describes the battle that goes on within us between our soul and the Spirit of God inside us:

> For those who are according to the flesh and are controlled by its unholy desires set their minds on and pursue those things which gratify the flesh, but those who are according to the Spirit and are controlled by the desires of the Spirit set their minds on and seek those things which gratify the [Holy] Spirit. Now the mind of the flesh [which is sense and reason without the Holy Spirit] is death [death that comprises all the miseries arising from sin, both here and hereafter]. But the mind of the [Holy] Spirit is life and [soul] peace [both now and forever]. [That is] because the mind of the flesh [with its carnal thoughts and purposes] is hostile to God, for it does not submit itself to God's Law; indeed it cannot. So then those who are living the life of the flesh [catering to the appetites and impulses of

their carnal nature] cannot please or satisfy God, or be
acceptable to Him. (AMP)

Our soul is a very powerful part of us. It can produce an emotion
or desire so strong within us that we can set our will to do almost
anything. This is why we often make wrong choices that were fueled
by sudden impulses. We must learn to recognize the "voice "of our
soul in order to walk in victory. Anything that brings defeat has to
originate out of your soul, because there is nothing that can defeat
or overcome the Spirit of God inside of you, for "He who is in you
is greater than he who is in the world" (1 John 4:4).

Before we were born again, most of our decisions were based on
information from our soul. Our desires were aroused sexually, so to
fulfill this desire we had sex. We were depressed, so we took a pill,
smoked a joint, or had a drink. We were hurt, so we retaliated by
lashing out or withdrawing from that individual. If you are a born-
again child of God with His Spirit living inside you, there can be
only one reason for failure: you have wrong information stored in
you, and you are acting on that wrong information.

Our minds are phenomenal pieces of tissue. They are like a mini-
computer that has enough memory to store all information that one
has fed it through visual and audio contact. It even takes all our
experiences and archives them for future withdrawals. It has the
ability to reason and analyze all information. It can think and help
us to make decisions. It can even visualize past experiences as well
as envision things in the future. Scientist tells us that we use only a
very small portion of this amazing computer. Doctors tell us that a
fetus inside the womb has information programmed into their tiny,
undeveloped minds to the point they jump at loud noises, respond to
our voices, and even feel rejection from those in the outside world.

Our minds store information from two sources: Information that is programmed when we are in a conscious state comes through general knowledge taught and observed, traditions, environment, and culture. The other source is our subconscious. Conscious thinking quits when you quit thinking. Your subconscious never rests, even when you are asleep. They say that 80 to 85 percent of brain activity takes place in the subconscious. Think about your dreams. You dream about things from your past or about what you recently heard or experienced. Psalms 16:7 says, "I will bless the Lord who has given me counsel; My heart also instructs me in the night seasons." I used to dream horrible dreams that were fearful, lustful, evil, but I've learned during the day to program my mind with praise, worship, and the Word. Remember that God told Joshua, "If you want to be successful, then meditate in the Word night and day "(Joshua 1:8 my paraphrase). Some of the most profound things in my life have happened when God awakened me with a thought, an idea, or His voice. Many times I have gotten up to write down a thought or pray and listen to His voice.

The information that we have stored through our conscious and subconscious determine who we are. It becomes our belief system. Our beliefs aren't necessarily the truth; they are our version of what we *believe* to be true. Many times these beliefs are programmed into our belief center through authoritative figures. They may be parents, teachers, professors, or peers. These beliefs will determine if we are led by our soul, or by the Spirit of God.

They also tell us how we view others. I was raised in a racist home; my parents thought people of other races were inferior, creating the belief in me. Also, we didn't attend church, and I came to the conclusion that Christians were weak and not very manly. Often authority figures also program into us how we are to treat our spouses and how we view right and wrong. Pastors often program us into how we view the Word of God. Some teach that God is against prosperity, that healing is no longer for us, or that we are to live a defeated life, looking for our rewards only when we get to heaven. They try to tell us that the power of God is not for today, that baptism in the Holy Spirit is no longer needed, that the gifts of God went out with the apostles. It is time to reprogram our belief center with who the Word of God says we are and what it says we can do as those that are recreated in His image. Paul said this: "You ran well. Who hindered you from obeying the truth? This persuasion does not come from Him who calls you" (Galatians 5:7–8).

Our belief systems are continually being programmed with what we hear. Music is very powerful tool. I love country western music, but several years ago I quit listening to it because I became aware that I would constantly be running horrible lyrics through my mind, such as "heaven's just a sin away" or "I'm a cheatin', drinkin' kinda man." Psychologists have discovered that continually watching violence through TV, movies, and video games has birthed violent crimes. Viewing pornography has bound many to sexual addictions, even to the point of rape and child molestation.

Our belief system is also programmed through things we experience. Those that go through failures in relationships often see themselves as failures, and they avoid any type of commitment. Some that failed in business ventures give up on the idea of being successful. Christians even have given up believing God cares and answers prayers, because of past faith failures.

When we continually program things into our belief systems, they eventually become so embedded they will become a stronghold. A stronghold is built from continually layering our beliefs until they are so embedded in us that we perceive them to be the truth. A stronghold built on lies often prevents us from accepting God's Words as the truth. The Greek word for *stronghold* is *ochuroma*, which means a fortress, prison, or military installation. A stronghold is good if it is built on truth, but if built on wrong information, it must be uprooted from our belief system.

The apostle Paul wrote, "For the weapons of our warfare are not physical [weapons of flesh and blood], but they are mighty before God for the overthrow and destruction of strongholds, [Inasmuch as we] refute arguments and theories and reasonings and every proud and lofty thing that sets itself up against the [true] knowledge of God; and we lead every thought and purpose away captive into the obedience of Christ (the Messiah, the Anointed One)" (2 Corinthians 10:4–5 AMP).

For us to reprogram our belief system, we must begin by deleting all information that doesn't line up with the Word of God. I was saved when I was twenty-eight years old. From the time I was able to make decisions as a child, everything I did was based on what was programmed into my belief system. As I grew into adolescence, if I had a desire, I acted on that desire. If I faced an obstacle, I used information from past experiences and acquired knowledge to see if it was possible. When we are born again, God transfers us from kingdom of darkness into His kingdom. We are no longer bound to the world, even though we live in it; we are residents of a higher realm. Many Christians fail because they enter into this new kingdom as priests and kings yet still try to operate out of the old system. They make choices based on their knowledge that was programmed into their belief system over many years. That is why it is often hard for us to move into the faith realm; for us to believe, we must first experience it, see it, or feel it. We have difficulty conquering certain sins because our desires overwhelm us, because we've never been freed from them.

Romans 12:2 says, "Do not be conformed to this world (this age), [fashioned after and adapted to its external, superficial customs], but be transformed (changed) by the [entire] renewal of your mind [by its new ideals and its new attitude], so that you may prove [for yourselves] what is the good and acceptable and perfect will of God, even the thing which is good and acceptable and perfect [in His sight for you]" (AMP). Strongholds in our lives must be pulled down and destroyed. They cannot be denied or covered up, because under the right conditions, they will rebuild.

Begin casting down those thoughts that do not line up with God's Word. Deny those things that we refer to as our flesh, and they will begin to shrivel up and die for lack of nourishment. Begin to find out who you are in Him, what belongs to you through Him and what you can do through Him. Reprogram your belief system through meditating on, studying, and acting on the Word of God.

Chapter 8

POSITIONED TO STAY AFLOAT

Some of the richest and most powerful people in the world partied and danced the night away on a luxurious ocean liner, unaware of the disaster and death awaiting them. On the morning of April 10, 1912, the *RMS Titanic* pulled away from the dock at Southampton, England, bound for New York City with 2,223 enthusiastic and excited passengers aboard. *Titanic* means "of great force." She was the largest luxury liner built at that time. The *Titanic* had all the amenities that even the finest hotels lacked: luxurious staterooms, swimming pools, restaurants, a hospital, and even a gymnasium.

As the *Titanic* eased out of Southampton's harbor, the excited passengers waved to family and friends standing on the deck as bands played and flags flew. Children ran and laughed along the pier as the great ship pulled away, blowing her whistle. As she made her turn toward the open waters, the passengers strolled on the decks, toured the staterooms, and stood in awe of her magnificent ballrooms. Her ornate beauty was the talk of the passengers, and her owners and designers described her as "unsinkable." The party atmosphere throughout the ship enthralled most of the passengers, while a few comfortably slept in the down-filled beds. Then, at 11:40 p.m., the *Titanic* was jolted as she crashed into a huge iceberg, causing her rivets to pop, ripping her bulkhead, allowing thousands of gallons of freezing water to fill the lower decks. As guests began to scream in panic and deckhands scurried to resolve the problems, the great lady began to gasp and sink into the icy sea. The death toll was 1,522—the worst maritime disaster in history.

The Word of God clearly teaches us that the last days will be "perilous times" when many will depart the faith … …many will sink. Matthew 24:37–39 says, "But as the days of Noah were, so also will the coming of the Son of Man be. For as in the days before the flood, they were eating and drinking, marrying and giving in marriage, until the day that Noah entered the ark, and did not know until the flood came and took them all away, so also will the coming of the Son of Man be." The "icebergs" of busyness have crashed into many lives, sweeping them to their deaths. The waves of apathy and complacency have pulled once mighty warriors for God to the bottom of the sea. The ocean floors of desires have reached up and grasped the faithful saints and pulled them into their seductive places of darkness.

I wish I could tell you that when you become a Christian, you will no longer face another trial. You will face storms that have the potential to wipe you out, but if you know how to position yourself, you will sail right through the storm with victory. What can we learn from the sinking of the *RMS Titanic* that we can apply to our lives so when storms come, we are able to ride them out without any damage to our lives?

The steel plate used for the hull of the *Titanic* was one and a half inches thick. A detailed analysis of small pieces from the wrecked hull revealed that it was made of a combination of metals that deforms and becomes brittle in cold or icy water, leaving it vulnerable to dent-induced ruptures. In other words, the makeup of this particular steel was not suitable for the conditions the *Titanic* was traveling in. We must make sure that our faith is built on a foundation that will withstand all the elements that the world and the enemy can bring against us. We must be strong in the Lord and resilient against temptation.

Outwardly the Titanic looked *invulnerable*. Some Christians are like that: outwardly they look strong, but inwardly there is no strength to withstand the attacks of the enemy. As Jesus said, "How horrible it will be for you, scribes and Pharisees! You hypocrites! You are like whitewashed graves that look beautiful on the outside but inside are full of dead people's bones and every kind of impurity. So on the outside you look as though you have God's approval, but inside you are full of hypocrisy and lawlessness" (Matthew 23:27–28 GWT).

To withstand outward attacks that try to drown us, we must be strong inwardly, being built on the foundation of Jesus Christ, our chief cornerstone. Ephesians 6:10–11 tells us, "Finally, my brethren, be strong in the Lord and in the power of His might. Put on the whole armor of God, that you may be able to stand against the wiles of the devil." When we are positioned in *Him,* we are strengthened; outside of Him, we are weakened. We are more than conquerors in Him (Romans 8:37). And Philippians 4:13 says, "I can do all things through Christ who strengthens me." My strength to overcome anything I face comes from Him and Him alone. When I'm out of position, I am vulnerable to the attacks of the enemy and the pull of the world. I get in position and remain in position through righteousness by obedience to His voice and His Word.

Insignificant Things Are Important

The *Titanic* was held together by tens of thousands of rivets that steelworkers used to piece her magnificent body together with. A rivet is minute compared to a ship, but it keeps the ship together. The builders had to remain on a very precise budget. As prices and labor costs began to escalate, they had to find ways to cut costs. Maybe they could have used lower-cost lights in the ballroom instead of the costly crystal chandeliers, or instead of using expensive imported woods for the railings and paneling, they might have used domestic wood. But rather than sacrifice what most would have noticed, they used low-cost—and low-quality—rivets. They looked like high-quality rivets, so no one would ever notice they contained slag, an impurity that caused them to break more easily.

Song of Solomon 2:15 says, "Catch us the foxes, the little foxes that spoil the vines." Often it's not the big things that destroy us, but rather a continual buildup of little things. A brass fixture does not tarnish overnight, but if it is not polished and cared for; it will lose its shine. The New Testament equivalent is found in 1 Corinthians 5:6: "Your glorying is not good. Do you not know that a little leaven leavens the whole lump?" Sin in our lives, if not dealt with through repentance, will eventually bring destruction to us. There are some that claim that Christians never need to repent after they have been saved. If allowed to remain in our lives, sin will eventually build up to the point that we no longer feel convicted by it. Forgiveness frees us from our sin, but repentance is what removes it from our lives.

The "little things" that may seem insignificant to our spiritual walk have great importance. Fellowship with other believers strengthens us, and we are to strengthen others by our testimonies and words of encouragement. Fellowship also places us in accountability to others. Just knowing that we are accountable to someone else can keep us from weakening. Our worship should not be limited to a Sunday morning service, but should be an attitude of heart continually, because when we are worshiping Him, we are drawn into His presence. Prayer and meditation on His Word build up our inner man. The implanted Word that we have meditated on comes forth out of our inner beings when we are facing a disaster. I cannot count the times that a certain Scripture has risen up within me when I have faced a situation that could sink me. I would grasp that Scripture, meditate on it, and confess it until I received the victory.

They Could Not See What They Were Headed Into

In the early 1900s, radar equipment had not been developed, and there was no GPS to direct them. It was standard procedure to place men in a high position, called a crow's nest, to scan the horizon for oncoming ships or natural obstructions. Normally the two men who were stationed in the crow's nest would have been equipped with binoculars. Why they didn't have them at this time is unknown. John 16:13 says, "But when He, the Spirit of Truth (the Truth-giving Spirit) comes, He will guide you into all the Truth (the whole, full Truth). For He will not speak His own message [on His own authority]; but He will tell whatever He hears [from the Father; He will give the message that has been given to Him], and He will announce and declare to you the things that are to come [that will happen in the future]" (AMP). The Holy Spirit is our radar and GPS. He warns us about things that will cause us to stumble and fall, and He directs our paths if we listen to and follow His voice.

Wrong Information

In those days it was standard procedure when sailing in Artic waters for the crew to lower a special bag to gather water for a temperature reading. The *Titanic*'s deck was much higher off the water than any other ship to date; therefore, the rope, which was standard issue, was way too short to drop the sack into the water. The crew thought it unnecessary to find a longer rope, so they used drinking water for their tests.

The next error occurred because the Marconi wireless operators, Jack Phillips and Harold Bride, thought it was unnecessary to relay information of icebergs in the area to Captain Edward Smith. *Deception* sinks many of God's children. Many times over, Jesus warned about not being deceived in the last days. The apostle Paul also warned many times to beware of deception. Deception simply believes a lie to be the truth. It was the tool Satan used to cause the fall of man in the Garden of Eden. And it is a very powerful thing. I've had pastor friends that got caught up in adultery and believed it was from God. Talking to them was like talking to a brick wall.

I've seen many Christians going the wrong way, but human words could not get them to see the error; only the power of the Holy Spirit can break deception. Many churches today want to be "seeker friendly," preaching grace to the point that people believe they can live how they want without repercussions. Here are two other popular deceptions: You can have all the blessings of God by just being His child. You can have divine favor in your life because you are under the new covenant.

Deception is simply being given the wrong information and acting on it. When we are told that we no longer have to ask God for forgiveness when we sin, we are being given the wrong information. When we are told that healing is not for today, we are being given the wrong information. You *cannot* live however you want, because the Bible says that the "wages of sin is death" (Romans 6:23). Yes, you can have the blessings of God all over your life; you can have His favor all over you; you can triumph over all enemies—but you *must* position yourself in *righteousness* by living in *obedience* to His Word.

They Were Unable to Turn to Avoid Disaster

The *Titanic* had three turbines to propel her across the ocean and a rudder that could change her course. By design, the builders failed to give the center turbine the capability of reversing. This feature would have allowed the captain to turn his ship much quicker, and it very possibly could have missed the iceberg. Hebrews 4:12 says, "For the Word that God speaks is alive and full of power [making it active, operative, energizing, and effective]; it is sharper than any two-edged sword, penetrating to the dividing line of the breath of life (soul) and [the immortal] spirit, and of joints and marrow [of the deepest parts of our nature], exposing and sifting and analyzing and judging the very thoughts and purposes of the heart" (AMP). The Word of God is alive and is a sharp sword meant to pierce our conscience to the point that we are convicted of and sorrowful for our sins. The Word is our standard for living; any time our lives get outside the perimeters of the Word, the Holy Spirit convicts us—not to condemn us, but to steer us away from eternal judgment. Repentance is God's way of reversing our course when we are headed in the wrong direction.

They Failed to Call for Help

Policy in those days was for all ships to cut off their radios at midnight. The *Titanic* hit the iceberg at 11:40 p.m. By the time they realized the tremendous danger they were facing, all radios of other ships had gone silent. The *USS California* was within ten miles of them, and had they know, they could have been there in minutes to assist and to take on passengers. Firing red flares is an international warning of emergency. In the excitement of preparing for her maiden cruise, the crew failed to load any flares.

Psalms 107:6 says this: "In their distress they cried out to the LORD. He rescued them from their troubles" (GWT). Aren't you glad that when you do hit a hard spot, you can call on God, your Deliverer? Also, we are to be His lifeline to those who are perishing. Many times, because of shame or not wanting to bother someone with their problems, Christians fail to call out to others. But we should be able to see signs that someone is drowning. Their joy has been swallowed up; their countenance shows depression. They are no longer faithfully at church. The confession of their mouth has become negative; there is an air of bitterness and hardness about them. We as children of God are to rescue the perishing.

They Were Not Prepared for a Disaster

On board that day were 2,223 passengers plus crew. Sadly, the ship had only enough lifeboat space for 1,178 people. Statistics tell us that every person or someone close to him or her will face a major disaster every five years. You cannot build a safety net in the midst of your ship sinking. Jesus taught a parable about two men who built houses (Luke 6:48–49). One man was so busy with life and other things that he began to cut corners. He thought it unnecessary to build a good foundation, because it took too much effort. The other man believed he needed to be prepared, so he built his house on rock. When the floods came, the house built on a good foundation withstood the storm; the other was destroyed. One never knows what tomorrow brings, but if you are grounded in the Word of God, you will soar through a storm, feast in a famine, and fly through a fire. You can make yourself *unsinkable*.

Chapter 9

POSITIONED TO REIGN

The old prophet drove his heifer toward the city of Bethlehem, thinking of the word God had spoken to him. Saul was king of Israel, but because of his disobedience to God's command, God no longer recognized him as king. Samuel's mission was to go to Bethlehem and anoint the one God had chosen to replace Saul as king. This chosen one was to come from the household of Jesse.

As Samuel entered the city, the leaders rushed toward the prophet to inquire why he was coming to their city. Samuel did not reveal his mission, but only informed them he was bringing a heifer to sacrifice unto the Lord. Jesse and seven of his sons were among the crowd that day. Immediately Samuel's eyes were drawn toward a man whose physical stature stood out from the rest of the crowd. Samuel gazed up and down on the man, visualizing him in a purple, gold-trimmed robe with a golden, jeweled crown on his head. He could see this powerful man leading his army into battle on a great white stallion with his blood-stained sword in his hand.

But the voice of God interrupted Samuel's thoughts, saying, "This is not the one." Samuel stood with his flask of oil in his hand, ready to anoint the one God had chosen to lead Israel. Samuel paused in front of Eliab, then Abinadab, then Shammah, and then four others, waiting for God to say, "Anoint." But there was no response from God. *Did I miss it?* Samuel thought. Often we think if it is not logical or feasible; then it must not be God and we *missed it*. Slowly he turned toward Jesse and asked, "Is this all the young men?" Jesse replied, "Well, there is one more," thinking his youngest son was too young and surely not qualified for such an important thing as being anointed by the great prophet Samuel.

David, the youngest, was out in the pasture, tending his father Jesse's sheep, making sure they didn't wander off where they would be easy prey for a predator. With his shepherd's staff, he moved them to a stream to drink and then eased them back to lush green grass to graze before taking them back into the pens to bed down for the night.

David looked up when he heard his brother call. As they walked back to his home, his brother explained the reason he was needed. When they reached where the crowd had gathered, David made his way through to where his father stood. Samuel looked at the young man standing at his father's side, thinking surely this was not the one. He was too young, not yet developed into manhood. But Samuel's thoughts were interrupted by the voice of God: "'Arise, anoint him; for this is the one!' Then Samuel took the horn of oil and anointed David in the midst of his brothers; and the Spirit of the LORD came upon David from that day forward" (1 Samuel 16:12–13). Before David was conceived, his *destiny* was to become a king.

Revelation 17:14 says, "For He is Lord of lords and King of kings." A king is one who has complete authority and dominion over a certain region. From His birth and the star that shined in the east, many thought that Jesus was the king of the Jews. When Jesus was taken before Pilate, He was asked, "Are you the King of the Jews?" (John 18:36).

Jesus answered, "My kingdom is not of this world. If My kingdom were of this world, My servants would fight, so that I should not be delivered to the Jews; but now My kingdom is not from here." Basically, there are only two kingdoms: the kingdom of God, often referred to as the kingdom of heaven, and the kingdom of darkness. When God created man, he gave him complete dominion and authority over every living thing on Earth. That included Satan and his company of fallen angels, whom God had exiled to this planet because of their rebellion against Him. Adam was as close to being God without being God as a mortal can be. He was *king* over the entire planet Earth. Everything on Earth was in subjection to him, but when he sinned, he immediately got out of *position* with God. Satan had stolen his kingship, and man went into exile. Adam was a king with no authority.

Ephesians 2:1–2 says, "And you were dead in your trespasses and sins in which you previously walked according to the ways of this world, according to the ruler who exercises authority over the lower heavens, the spirit now working in the disobedient" (Holman Christian Standard Bible). From the time that Adam fell in the garden (Genesis 3:13-15) satan *the prince of this world and ruler of the kingdom of darkness* began to expect the One (Jesus) to make an appearance on planet earth to completely annihilate his authority and power. It was this same ruler, or king, that recognized the ruler and kingship that Jesus operated under; therefore, his plan was to eliminate this king. First Corinthians 2:8 says, "which none of the rulers of this age knew; for had they known, they would not have crucified the Lord of glory."

Jesus is the "King of kings," signifying that He is the supreme *king*, and under His kingship are all other *kings* (plural).

It is yours and my *destiny* and *purpose* to be *kings*. As Revelation 5:9–10 says, "For You were slain, And have redeemed us to God by Your blood Out of every tribe and tongue and people and nation, And have made us kings and priests to our God; And we shall reign on the earth." God has *made* us to be kings. *To make* means to construct something with necessary and proper materials so that it functions according to its purpose. For a house to become a house, the builder must have a plan or blueprint with the finished product in mind. Jeremiah 29:11 says, "For I know the plans I have for you, declares the LORD, plans to prosper you and not to harm you, plans to give you hope and a future" (NIV).

Often we get locked into who we've *been* or who we *think* we are. Countless people come into our church who are homeless, addicted to drugs or alcohol, or broken by their circumstances. I love to watch them as God washes away their past and clothes them with robes of righteousness. I am always amazed when they get the revelation of who they are in Christ, because it completely revolutionizes their lives. If you've had a God encounter, the Bible says that you have become a *new creation:* "Therefore, if anyone is in Christ, he is a new creation; the old has gone, the new has come!" (2 Corinthians 5:17 NIV). God didn't remodel or refurbish you; He completely put new materials in you and now you are a new creation. Jesus told Nicodemus that unless "one is born of water and the Spirit, he cannot enter the kingdom of God."

Kings are not elected or appointed. In most cases, kingship comes through inheritance. It is passed down through birthright. When a king dies, the firstborn son becomes heir to the throne. A servant can never exercise kingship; it must come through birth.

> But when the fullness of the time had come, God sent forth His Son, born of a woman, born under the law, to redeem those who were under the law, that we might receive the adoption as sons. And because you are sons, God has sent forth the Spirit of His Son into your hearts,

> crying out, "Abba, Father!" Therefore you are no longer a
> slave but a son, and if a son, then an heir of God through
> Christ. (Galatians 4:4–7)

When you were *reborn*, God put His blood and His DNA inside you, and now you are a son and an heir of a king. You now have a legal right to reign on this earth. Your kingship is now, not later; it is here, not in heaven. You must learn how to *reign* on earth. Psalms 115:16 says, "The heavens are the LORD's, but the earth He has given to the human race" (HCSB).

His disciples recognized how all things on Earth were in subjection to him, so they asked. "How do we pray?" Jesus replied, "Therefore, you should pray like this: Our Father in heaven, Your name be honored as holy. Your kingdom come. Your will be done on earth as it is in heaven" (Matthew 6:9–10 HCSB). In verse 10, Jesus said we are to ask for His kingdom in heaven to come onto Earth. *Kingdom* is easily translated as a king's domain or realm of authority and dominion. As kings, we are simply to operate with authority and dominion over the whole earth, which includes all unseen powers and principalities of the kingdom of darkness. In the kingdom of heaven, sickness and disease do not exist. I believe it is God's will for you and me to not only be healed, but also to walk in divine health.

The exodus of the children of Israel was a shadow of people being born again and liberated from their old lives under the new covenant. The children that came out of bondage in Egypt came out lacking nothing. As servants in Egypt, they lived a very substandard life. They only had shelter and enough food to give them strength to labor from sunup to sundown. When they left Egypt, they left with the Egyptians' gold, silver, and fine clothing. Besides getting a complete reversal in their financial condition, they also had no sickness among them. That is quite a statement when you consider there were more than 2.5 million of them. As Psalms 105:37 says, "He also brought them out with silver and gold, and there was none feeble among His tribes."

We know that sickness and poverty does not exist in heaven. So if we are positioned in Him, living in righteousness and faithful in our tithes, as kings we can declare, "Sickness and lack, how dare you take up residence in the kingdom of God? Kingdom of heaven, come into our lives. Your *good* will comes to us." When Peter received the revelation of who Jesus was, the keys to operating under kingdom principles were given to him. Keys are symbolic of one having authority. And Jesus said, "I will give you the keys of the kingdom of heaven, and whatever you bind on earth will be bound in heaven, and whatever you loose on earth will be loosed in heaven" (Matthew 16:19).

The Greek word for *bind* means "to adhere" or "to tie up." And the word for *loose* means "to destroy or crush." Note also that *heaven* here is not referring to the abode of God, but to the heavenlies where the prince of the air (Satan) has dominion (Ephesians 2:2). When you are reigning in life as a king, you can use the keys of the kingdom and can loose the addiction that has you bound, the habit or sin that has kept hanging on. You've prayed and kept praying, yet you still cannot resist that temptation. Now that you are in position with God, you can command that thing to be loosed from you. Jesus used His kingly authority to heal a woman that was crippled:

> Now He was teaching in one of the synagogues on the Sabbath. And behold, there was a woman who had a spirit of infirmity eighteen years, and was bent over and could in no way raise herself up. But when Jesus saw her, He called her to Him and said to her, "Woman, you are loosed from your infirmity." And He laid His hands on her, and immediately she was made straight, and glorified God. (Luke 13:10–13)

With the *authority* you have as a king, you can command that bondage to be broken, "for sin shall not have dominion over you, for you are not under law but under grace" (Romans 6:14). When you and I get the revelation of who we are in Christ, we will begin to have dominion instead of circumstances having dominion over us. I continually hear Christians saying, "I can't." A king has the authority to decree something and turn it in to "it will be done." It is God's will for his kingdom to be birthed and exercised on Earth through earthly kings: you and me.

Next in the Lord's Prayer, Jesus said we are to ask that God's will, or His desire that is in heaven be manifest here on Earth. It is God's will for you to be healed and in health, for you to be completely free from any sin, addiction, and infirmity, and to be successful and prosperous in all that you do. He made you to be a *king*. When you are positioned *with Him*, you can reign *with Him*. So the next time the enemy invades your turf, use the authority that God has given you and put the enemy in subjection to your rule.

When we look at the ministry of Jesus, we see where people are healed from various diseases, freed from various infirmities and bondages, raised from the dead, and given eternal life. Do you realize that Jesus never once taught about how to be saved, how to be delivered, how to heal someone, or how to live in prosperity? Look at the basis of His ministry:

> And Jesus went about all Galilee, teaching in their synagogues, preaching the gospel of the kingdom, and healing all kinds of sickness and all kinds of disease among the people. Then His fame went throughout all Syria; and they brought to Him all sick people who were afflicted with various diseases and torments, and those who were demon-possessed, epileptics, and paralytics; and He healed them. (Matthew 4:23–24)

Jesus preached and taught about the *kingdom*, and after the people heard, He healed and delivered all those He taught. In fact, Jesus primarily taught about the kingdom of God or heaven. This was so important that He taught it 129 times in the Gospels and even taught it after He was resurrected from the dead. "He also presented Himself alive after His suffering by many infallible proofs, being seen by them during forty days and speaking of the things pertaining to the kingdom of God" (Acts 1:3). It seems that Jesus was trying to get a point across since most of the parables were about the *kingdom*. Whether he taught in the synagogues or on a seashore, He taught about the kingdom; therefore we must surmise that we are to reign as kings.

Luke 4:18–19 records Jesus as saying,

> "The Spirit of the Lord [is] upon Me, because He has anointed Me [the Anointed One, the Messiah] to preach the good news (the Gospel) to the poor; He has sent Me to announce release to the captives and recovery of sight to the blind, to send forth as delivered those who are oppressed [who are downtrodden, bruised, crushed, and broken down by calamity], To proclaim the accepted and acceptable year of the Lord [the day when salvation and the free favors of God profusely abound]." (AMP)

When Jesus preached and taught about the kingdom of God/heaven, people were healed and delivered. Look how teaching about the kingdom of God goes hand in hand with that authority and dominion of a king:

> And He descended to Capernaum, a town of Galilee, and there He continued to teach the people on the Sabbath days. And they were amazed at His teaching, for His word was with authority and ability and weight and power.

Now in the synagogue there was a man who was possessed by the foul spirit of a demon; and he cried out with a loud (deep, terrible) cry, Ah, let us alone! What have You to do with us [What have we in common], Jesus of Nazareth? Have You come to destroy us? I know Who You are—the Holy One of God! But Jesus rebuked him, saying, be silent (muzzled, gagged), and come out of him! And when the demon had thrown the man down in their midst, he came out of him without injuring him in any possible way. And they were all amazed and said to one another, What kind of talk is this? For with authority and power He commands the foul spirits and they come out! And a rumor about Him spread into every place in the surrounding country. Then He arose and left the synagogue and went into Simon's (Peter's) house. Now Simon's mother-in-law was suffering in the grip of a burning fever, and they pleaded with Him for her. And standing over her, He rebuked the fever, and it left her; and immediately she got up and began waiting on them. Now at the setting of the sun [indicating the end of the Sabbath], all those who had any [who were] sick with various diseases brought them to Him, and He laid His hands upon every one of them and cured them. And demons even came out of many people, screaming and crying out, You are the Son of God! But He rebuked them and would not permit them to speak, because they knew that He was the Christ (the Messiah). And when daybreak came, He left [Peter's house] and went into an isolated [desert] place. And the people looked for Him until they came up to Him and tried to prevent Him from leaving them. But He said to them, I must preach the good news (the Gospel) of the kingdom of God to the other cities [and towns] also, for I was sent for this [purpose].

Several years ago, we took the girls to the Broadmoor Hotel in Colorado Springs, Colorado, for Christmas. This is a very old and prestigious hotel in the foothills of the Rocky Mountains. Lou Ann and the girls had looked forward to this trip for months. At Christmastime, the hotel and all the grounds are extravagantly decorated. All the trees are lit up, and it is quite a beautiful sight. They do a dinner show about a Rocky Mountain Christmas. There were ice skating exhibitions and a show by the Olympians who trained in Colorado Spring.

Lou Ann started feeling ill when we arrived. She loves to shop and was looking forward to all the shopping districts, but that day she decided to spend much of the time in the car as I took the girls into all the shops. The night of the play, she began to run a high fever, so she went back to the room. In the middle of the night, the heat coming from her body awakened me. I rose up, put my hand on her, and commanded the fever to leave. Lou Ann said that her body began to cool, layer by layer. In a matter of seconds, the fever had left her body. She slept soundly from then on and awoke completely healed ready to enjoy the rest of our vacation.

When we begin to *receive* and *walk* in kingdom-of-God principles, we not only receive healing, deliverance, and prosperity, but we also impart salvation, healing, deliverance, and prosperity to others. Sickness, disease, and bondage from the enemy will be subject to our kingly authority. Jesus says, "And as you go, preach, saying, 'The kingdom of heaven is at hand.' Heal the sick, cleanse the lepers, raise the dead, cast out demons. Freely you have received, freely give" (Matthew 10:7–8). The kingdom is not far off in distance or time; kingdom reign is available now for those that position themselves in righteousness.

In recent days, we have seen rulers exiled from their kingdoms. Saddam Hussein, the ruthless leader of Iraq, was ousted from his luxurious palace by our troops, later to be found hidden in a hole. Hosni Mubarak from Egypt and Muammar Gaddafi of Libya were stripped of their authority and live in exile. They no longer have the right to live in luxury; they have no power in their kingdoms; they can no longer bring change by their words; and they are no longer recognized by the world as "kings" of their nations. Hussein was found guilty and executed, Gaddafi was beaten and shot by rebel leaders, and Mubarak was sentenced to life imprisonment.

Are you an exiled king, a child through inheritance that is living outside the promises and authority of God? Matthew 4:17 says, "From that time Jesus began to preach, crying out, Repent (change your mind for the better, heartily amend your ways, with abhorrence of your past sins), for the kingdom of heaven is at hand" (AMP). Kingdom authority is available to you and me—*if* we *position* ourselves in *righteousness*. To become kings, there must be a turning in our lives. Righteousness is a lifestyle of holiness, where one is being victorious over sin. You cannot reign like a king if you are living like the prodigal son, who walked away from his kingdom to live a life separated from his father and to live a lifestyle he desired. When he realized where he was and how far he had fallen, he made a *turn around* and went back to his father's house. When he arrived there, his father met him, put his arms around him, and placed a robe on him and a ring on his finger, signifying he was restored to his kingship. If you will see where you are now and turn back to your heavenly Father, He will greet you with open arms, forgive you, and place the anointing of king on you.

Romans 14:17 says, "[After all] the kingdom of God is not a matter of [getting the] food and drink [one likes], but instead it is righteousness (that state which makes a person acceptable to God) and [heart] peace and joy in the Holy Spirit" (AMP). We must have a turning of our mindset. Mephibosheth, the son of Jonathon and grandson of King Saul, was heir to his father's land, servants, and home. During a battle where his father and Saul were killed, Mephibosheth was crippled and abandoned. When King David found Mephibosheth, living in exile, he took him to the palace, telling him that all belonged to him. Mephibosheth replied, "Why would you even look at a dead dog like me?" (see 2 Samuel 9:1–11).

As long as you keep looking at your past—at what you've obtained and what you've accomplished—and seeing that is all you can ever be, you will never become a king. If you feel you will never go beyond what you are doing now, you will never be a king. You must realize that Jesus is King of kings, and you are one of those kings, because he has made you a king to reign on this earth. Put on the robe of righteousness, take your scepter in your hand (your Bible), and declare that Jesus the King of kings has given you a kingdom on this earth. Your kingdom is your home, your workplace, and your play place. In fact, everywhere you go is your kingdom.

So take the authority that Jesus restored to you and change the world around you instead of allowing circumstances to reign over you. Get into position as king, and decree that you are an overcomer, that you will reign and rule in your life. Command sickness, poverty, depression, and any other circumstance to bow at your command.

Chapter 10

POSITIONED TO WITHSTAND THE STORM

Sunday afternoon February 27, 2011, was a beautiful day in Austin, Texas, with sunshine and a light breeze. Lou Ann and I had just finished a round of golf at the beautiful Barton Creek Resort on the outskirts of our former hometown. We had gone there for few days to golf and relax, commemorating our wedding anniversary.

We were about ten miles away from the hotel and eight hours from home when Lou Ann received a phone call from a neighbor asking if we were okay, because she could see a major wildfire headed straight toward our home. Lou Ann informed her that we were out of town, thanked her for the call, and hung up. And we immediately began to pray.

After a few moments, realizing that it would be at least seven hours before we could be back, I asked Lou Ann to phone our son-in-law, Jeff, who was on the Randall County volunteer fire department. He answered his phone, which was amazing because he was fighting a fire that was completely engulfing the house across the street from ours. We had just completed a major remodel on our house, which is in a gated area in a very rugged but beautiful canyon that's part of Palo Dura Canyon State Park. The drought of 2011 had just begun in the late fall, and the tall grass, junipers, and mesquites were ready fuel for the fire. It had ignited about a quarter of a mile away from our home and was driven by sixty-nine mile-per-hour winds.

Lou Ann asked Jeff, "What's going on with the fire?" Jeff's answer was not what we were ready to hear. He said that they had already declared the home across the street from us a total loss. A whirlwind of flames had jumped his truck and headed toward our house, consuming our cedar stay entrance and burning our Texas flag, which sat on top of a thirty-foot flagpole that was being whipped by the powerful wind. Jeff went on to say that it looked like our house was gone also.

After she hung up, we began to pray intensely in the Spirit for the next hour. Realizing it was in God's hands, not ours, we stopped in Llano for lunch. The next report we got from Jeff came after the fire trucks were able to make it up our circular drive. He said it looked as though God had erected a steel fence around our home. The flames consumed our yard, scorched the bushes next to the house, burnt a portion of our backyard fence, and even burned a horseshoe ring around my tractor and new flatbed trailer.

By next morning this massive wildfire had consumed thirty-two homes, forty other structures, and several thousand acres before firefighters could get it under control. But not a spark had touched our home—not even the dry wood shake roof. What a mighty God we serve!

We have all seen in recent years how natural events can be very destructive. The tsunami that hit Japan in March 2011 killed tens of thousands and destroyed hundreds of homes and business. The massive tornado, whose mile-wide path tore through Joplin, Missouri, in May, 2011, left 141 dead and damage in the billions of dollars. Fortunately modern technology enables us to predict, track, and monitor these events to some extent, giving us foreknowledge so we can prepare. Tsunamis can be predicted through seismic waves on the ocean floor; tornadoes can be predicted often an hour or so in advance; and hurricanes can be monitored and tracked days in advance, giving those in their paths time to prepare for safety.

Unfortunately, the storms of life often come suddenly and unexpected, with no sign of their coming. In Matthew 8 the disciples had been in a great meeting with Jesus, where many were healed and delivered. Then Jesus gave the command to "go to the other side" (Matthew 8:18). Let's look at this same account in the Gospel of Mark: "On that same day [when] evening had come, He said to them, Let us go over to the other side [of the lake]. And leaving the throng, they took Him with them, [just] as He was, in the boat [in which He was sitting]. And other boats were with Him. And a furious storm of wind [of hurricane proportions] arose, and the waves kept beating into the boat, so that it was already becoming filled" (Mark 4:35–37 AMP). This was not just a gale and rough seas; this storm was of the magnitude of a hurricane that came out of nowhere. Matthew 8:24 says that "suddenly a great tempest arose on the sea."

Like the disciples, we often sail pleasantly through a life with no ripples—and *suddenly* a phone call or a conversation is like a great wind arising and pushing waves toward us. There's been an accident, someone died, you are overdrawn, I want a divorce, you've been laid off, or the report shows cancer. None of us is immune to life's storms, but I do believe that it is God's will to guide us around them. God knows what's on the horizon, and many storms can be avoided by *positioning* ourselves in Him by staying in His will, both listening and obeying His voice.

Storms that we bring upon ourselves are "storms of judgment." Proverbs 26:2 says that "a curse without cause shall not alight." In other words, there may be a reason behind your storm. God did not create, but He allowed it. God's judgment can come as a gentle breeze that blows away your opportunities and that directs His favor and blessings away from you. Psalms 9:16 says that, "the LORD is known for his justice. The wicked are trapped by their own deeds." That Scripture is followed by the word *Meditation*, which is a note to the reader to think about that.

God never desires bad to come toward us, but when we become disobedient to His Word, we can expect His judgment. In Zechariah 7 we see that when God's people refused to obey, His judgment came upon them: "But they refused to heed, shrugged their shoulders, and stopped their ears so that they could not hear. Yes, they made their hearts like flint, refusing to hear the law and the words which the LORD of hosts had sent by His Spirit through the former prophets. Thus great wrath came from the LORD of hosts" (Zechariah 7:11–12). Hebrews 10 reminds us of the consequences of our sins, if not removed through forgiveness and repentance: "For we know Him who said, 'Vengeance is Mine, I will repay,' says the Lord. And again, 'The LORD will judge His people.' It is a fearful thing to fall into the hands of the living God" (vv. 30–31).

Yes, God will judge His people for their sins. One never knows when God's mercy and grace will end and His judgment begins. Like our weather forecasters, who warn us of storms headed our way, God's warning through His Holy Spirit is a sign of His judgment on the horizon. When you get into a storm of God's judgment, rebuking or praying will never get you out; only obedience and repentance can deliver you.

Jesus taught about preparing our lives, that when storms come we would survive them. He said,

> "Therefore everyone who hears these words of mine and
> puts them into practice is like a wise man who built his

house on the rock. The rain came down, the streams rose, and the winds blew and beat against that house; yet it did not fall, because it had its foundation on the rock. But everyone who hears these words of mine and does not put them into practice is like a foolish man who built his house on sand. The rain came down, the streams rose, and the winds blew and beat against that house, and it fell with a great crash." (Matthew 7:24–27 NIV)

The key words in this passage are not only building your life on solid foundation through a relationship with Him and His Word, but also *practicing,* or being a doer of what you hear (see James 1:22).

Many times you will face storms of adversity. The storm that the disciples in the boat faced was neither a storm of judgment nor a storm of purpose (which I will discuss later). This storm was birthed in sea of hell to destroy the disciples by drowning them or at least by getting them off their course. These types of storms often follow revelation or direction for your life. You might get a revelation from the Word of God that gives you both inspiration and direction to what God has for you. It may come through a message from the pulpit, a prophetic word, or a rhema word that arises in your spirit while meditating on His Word.

Often believers launch off into a deeper level of commitment, ministry, or calling when *suddenly* a storm arises to cause them to lose their vision or redirect their destiny. The storm may be a temptation to lure them away, or it may be a conversation or a report that disrupts and makes them want to give up; because the waves look overwhelming and the winds of resistance are too strong.

A man that once attended our church, but has since passed away, shared his story with me. J. lived most of his life in poverty and had a disease that kept him bed-bound much of his final years. He was born into a wealthy ranching family in the West. He spent his early years serving God in the church, and as a teenager he felt the call of God to preach. J. went through seminary and began pastoring churches. Soon he found himself pastoring a fairly large church in the city and a small church in a rural ranching community at the same time.

Life was going good for J. But one winter he developed a cough that wouldn't go away. One of his church members told him to try drinking a home remedy that was a mixture of whiskey, lemon juice, and honey. J. at first declined, saying that he had never drunk anything in his entire life that contained alcohol. But at the member's insistence, J. finally gave in and began using the concoction, not knowing the storm that loomed on the horizon.

J. began to acquire a taste for alcohol and the feeling it gave him. He began to drink more and more until his marriage broke up. His wife and children leaving him only caused him to drink more to ease the pain of his loss. J. was asked to resign his pastoral positions and soon found himself living on the streets, doing what he could to earn enough to buy another bottle of whiskey. J. finally ended up in a rehab center, where he was delivered from alcohol and learned a new trade. Even though J. never went back to alcohol, the storm had taken him off his course, and he often talked about missing what God had planned for him.

Storms often change the course of those in its path. Katrina, one of our nation's deadliest and costliest hurricanes, relocated many to other parts of the country. Lives and destinies have been altered because of storms. Death has stolen destinies; sickness and accidents have kept many from reaching their goals and dreams. Financial disasters have affected many. Affairs and addictions often alter courses for several generations.

Our choices dictate whether we reach the other side of our future. Deuteronomy 30:19–20 says, "This day I call heaven and earth as witnesses against you that I have set before you life and death, blessings and curses. Now choose life, so that you and your children may live and that you may love the LORD your God, listen to his voice, and hold fast to him. For the LORD is your life, and he will give you many years in the land he swore to give to your fathers, Abraham, Isaac and Jacob" (NIV). This storm was sent to disrupt the purpose Jesus had, for Jesus had said, "Let us go to the other side." Within those anointed words was enough power to take the disciples to the other side.

Did you notice that immediately after Jesus got into the boat, he lay down to take a nap? I don't believe the enemies' storm was a surprise to Jesus. He knows all things—past, present, and future. I believe He was just seeing if the disciples would apply what they had been taught, to see if their faith was real or superficial. To get through the storms of adversity you must *embrace the truth* by finding Scripture that applies to your situation, mediate on it, pray it, and don't let go of it through doubt and unbelief. *Faith* will always get you to the other side.

Born and raised in West Texas, part of Tornado Alley, I was used to the sirens going off in the middle of the night and breaking reports interrupting a TV program, informing listeners that there was either a tornado watch, meaning weather conditions were conducive for tornadoes, or a tornado warning, meaning funnel clouds had been sighted. In the springtime, storm chasers flock to our area like vultures hunting their prey. They place their lives in great danger, going through huge hailstorms, intense lightning, and torrential rainfall to gather information and film footage of the huge funnel-shaped rotating clouds that drop out of wall clouds, destroying everything in their paths like huge bulldozers. I've seen entire small towns completely leveled by their devastation.

It is hard to associate God with a storm of this nature, but Job 40 says that He spoke to Job from out of a whirlwind. Actually, when you study the word *whirlwind* in the Hebrew, it refers to a hurricane, which is also a rotating cloud—like a tornado at sea. In its very center, or the "eye," is complete tranquility. That's an odd place for God to speak from, but sometimes He uses a storm for his purpose.

Very little is known about Elijah, except that he was a mighty prophet of God. We know nothing of his family or his age. Second Kings 2:1 says, "And it came to pass, when the LORD was about to take up Elijah into heaven by a whirlwind, that Elijah went with Elisha from Gilgal." There are a few very interesting facts about this Scripture. First, this storm did not come by surprise. The sons of the prophets at Bethel and Elisha knew it was coming. "Now the sons of the prophets who were at Bethel came out to Elisha, and said to him, 'Do you know that the LORD will take away your master from over you today?' And he said, 'Yes, I know; keep silent!'" (v. 3). Second, the sons of the prophets who were at Jericho knew about it: "Then Elijah said to him, 'Elisha, stay here, please, for the LORD has sent me on to Jericho.' But he said, 'As the LORD lives, and as your soul lives, I will not leave you!' So they came to Jericho. Now the sons of the prophets who were at Jericho came to Elisha and said to him, 'Do you know that the LORD will take away your master from over you today?' So he answered, 'Yes, I know; keep silent!'" (vv. 4–5). In fact, even Elijah knew a storm was coming to take him: "And so it was, when they had crossed over, that Elijah said to Elisha, 'Ask! What may I do for you, before I am taken away from you?' Elisha said, 'Please let a double portion of your spirit be upon me'" (v. 9). I believe that if God is going to send a purpose-driven storm into your life, He will prepare you beforehand.

Many who read this account think God sent this storm to take Elijah because he failed the test by becoming afraid of Jezebel. God is not going to use a test to try to take you out. His tests are only meant to strengthen us, not to weaken us. There once was a famous violin maker from Europe whose violins were envied by his peers, not only for their magnificent heavenly tones but also for their incomparable beauty. When asked where he found such beautiful wood that emitted such marvelous sounds, he said he often watched other violin makers go into the valleys to pick the trees from which they formed their instruments. However, he said he climbed to the outcroppings on the mountaintops seeking trees that were twisted and gnarled by storms that encircled the higher elevations. He said, "The twisted grains and fibers caused by what the trees went through produces the sounds I am seeking." *Storms of purpose* are meant to prepare us to reach our potential.

> And so it was, when they had crossed over, that Elijah said to Elisha, "Ask! What may I do for you, before I am taken away from you?" Elisha said, "Please let a double portion of your spirit be upon me." So he said, You have asked a hard thing. Nevertheless, if you see me when I am taken from you, it shall be so for you; but if not, it shall not be so." Then it happened, as they continued on and talked, that suddenly a chariot of fire appeared with horses of fire, and separated the two of them; and Elijah went up by a whirlwind into heaven. (2 Kings 2:9–11)

Some storms are not meant to take you *out*, but to take you *up*. Elijah was one of only two people that never died; Enoch was the other. Elijah's storm took him to a place that not even death could touch. A storm of purpose is meant to take you to a level where sin that brings spiritual death cannot touch you. When God sends you through a storm of purpose, you will always have something to impart to others. From out of the storm Elijah thrust his mantle of anointing on Elisha.

Back to the disciples in the middle of a huge storm that was threatening their lives. They had pushed the panic button; fear was overcoming all their senses. A few years ago, a friend of mine was following me back from Benjamin, Texas. He was pulling a bumper-pull horse trailer carrying two large horses. I just happened to look in my rearview mirror to see his pickup take a hard left turn in the middle of nowhere. Sensing something wrong, I quickly hit speed-dial on my phone to call Lou Ann. I said, "Pray! Mike is in a storm." As soon as I uttered those few words, still looking in the mirror, I saw what looked like a tornado behind me. Dust blew as his truck and trailer rolled three times.

When I reached his truck, the trailer tires were spinning as it lay on its side. The horses were standing, shaking, in the bar ditch. Mike's red truck was upright, facing the opposite direction, with all the windows broken out. Mike was sitting there with a faraway look in his eyes, tightly gripping the steering wheel. I asked him if he was okay. Being a cowboy all of his life and ranch-raised, he replied, "My daddy always said, Son, if ever get in a wreck, take a deep seat and hold on."

In a storm, *stay in the boat*. The boat is not is not your enemy; it is your vehicle to safety. In any storm, being in the right position will determine if you will survive or be destroyed. Any time a storm is approaching our area; TV stations interrupt regular programming to let us know of potential danger. The Holy Spirit living in us warns of approaching dangers. We may be in a wrongful relationship, have a sin we haven't dealt with, or be complacent in serving God.

As the storm gets closer to our area, the newscasters again interrupt, telling us to take shelter immediately. No matter how big the storm is, God is our refuge and shelter. As long as the disciples were in the boat with Jesus, no power, principality, or storm could take them out. The church is our vehicle in the midst of storms, but some bail out at the slightest shaking in their lives.

Finally, in a storm, remember your destiny is on the other side, and it is God's desire that you reach it.

Chapter 11

POSITIONED FOR BATTLE

"The skillful fighter puts himself into a position
which makes defeat impossible and does not
miss the moment for defeating the enemy."
Sun Tze, *The Art of War*

From earliest times, leaders found they needed strategies of warfare to secure victories. Whether we are aware of it or not, we are in a battle against an enemy we cannot see or touch. This enemy is known by many names, but is usually referred to as Satan or the Devil. He has been around since the beginning of time. By nature he is an eternal spirit; in other words, he will always exist. In the beginning, he was in the presence of God.

> You were in Eden, the garden of God. Your clothing was adorned with every precious stone—red carnelian, pale-green peridot, white moonstone, blue-green beryl, onyx, green jasper, blue lapis lazuli, turquoise, and emerald—all beautifully crafted for you and set in the finest gold. They were given to you on the day you were created. I ordained and anointed you as the mighty angelic guardian. You had access to the holy mountain of God and walked among the stones of fire. You were blameless in all you did from

the day you were created until the day evil was found in you. (Ezekiel 28:13–15 NLT)

When pride filled Satan, he rebelled against God, so God cast him and one-third of the angels out of heaven onto this planet called Earth. His final destination is the "eternal lake of fire," along with those who followed him.

Satan is a spirit being; therefore, he cannot be seen with the naked eye unless he manifests himself in some manner. A few years ago I was aroused from sleep and sensed a presence on my bedroom. Our bed is next to patio doors; we usually sleep with curtains drawn to allow light into the room. When I rolled over, I was shocked to see a large figure standing between my bed and the patio doors. Immediately I knew it was not a heavenly angel but rather a demon or a "fallen angel." This figure was clothed in a dark robe with a hood. I could not make out any facial features. I quickly said, "In Jesus'—," and even before I could complete my sentence, it was gone. I got up and thought about this incident for a few minutes, and then returned to bed and peaceful sleep.

Another time I was dreaming what I later knew was a "spiritual" dream in which I was in a spiritual battle. I was struggling against a demonic force that was trying to come through my door. Finally I shouted in my dream, "I command you to leave now in Jesus' name." Suddenly Lou Ann and I were awakened by a loud noise, followed by a scratching sound. I turned on the lights to the bedroom and still heard the noise. On one of our bedroom walls was a very large painting swinging back and forth like a pendulum. A large eye screw had pulled loose, leaving the painting hanging from the large, twisted wire and a hook in the wall.

The Greek word for *spirit* is *pneuma,* which means "wind." Here in West Texas, we experience a lot of wind, especially in the springtime.

Winds gusting up to thirty miles per hour send dirt, debris, leaves, and tumbleweeds flying across parking lots, fields, and streets. You cannot see the wind, but you can see its effects. If you were to look inside an empty wind tunnel with winds above one hundred miles per hour, you could not see the wind. Wind is invisible. Satan and his demonic spirits are like that also. You cannot see them, but you can see their damage, such as premature death, poverty, destruction, sickness, disease, and addiction. Ephesians 6:12 says, "For we are not fighting against flesh-and-blood enemies, but against evil rulers and authorities of the unseen world, against mighty powers in this dark world, and against evil spirits in the heavenly places" (NLT).

Peter compares this unseen enemy, which comes to kill, steal, and destroy (John 10:10), to a roaring lion. First Peter 5:8 says, "Be well balanced (temperate, sober of mind), be vigilant and cautious at all times; for that enemy of yours, the devil, roams around like a lion roaring [in fierce hunger], seeking someone to seize upon and devour" (AMP). Peter uses the word *sober-minded* in contrast to a mind affected by alcohol. Even in moderation, alcohol dulls our senses and our ability to react.

One night, several years before I was saved, I exited a nightclub where I had been dancing with another man's girlfriend. As I walked around the corner of the building, the man hit me in the head with a beer bottle. I literally saw sparks. Being dazed, I watched as the man ran away. Being sober-minded means that we are always on the alert, because there is an enemy that stalks and waits to catch us off guard.

Peter also warns us to be vigilant and cautious at all times, because our adversary (opponent), the Devil, is seeking someone he can devour. Lions are very powerful animals, often weighing more than five hundred pounds and measuring four feet in height at their shoulders. They can reach speeds in excess of sixty miles per hour. Their prey is no match for their strength; their sharp teeth and powerful jaws can break bones and rip flesh from their victims. This is why they are called the "kings of the jungle."

Satan is like a roaring lion. Lions seldom attack large groups, but their roar can wreak havoc. Their main focus is on stragglers that fall behind from the herd or crowd. In the same way, the enemy is looking for ways to separate you from God, the one who empowers you with authority to defeat your enemy. Satan will get you busy to distract you from intimacy with God. He will attempt to cause you to be offended, so that you aren't involved in church. He will even tempt you to sin to separate you from God.

Sick and crippled animals cannot keep up with the rest of the herd, so they are vulnerable to lion attacks. Like a lion, Satan looks for the weak and the crippled—that is, those who lack knowledge of who they are in Christ, those who lack knowledge of the authority, dominion, and power living inside them. Satan looks for loners, those that are not connected to a body and those that choose friends that aren't following Christ. Satan looks for those that have been offended, hurt, or have become bitter. They are easy prey, because they are looking for an ear to hear their complaints. He looks for those who are out of position or living with unrepented sin.

We are only fooling ourselves if we expect God to bless and protect us if we have sin that has not been repented of and forgiven. Many Christians are great repeaters of sin. They sin and quickly ask God to forgive them in order to be back under His blessings and protection. But then they commit the same sin again. There is no repentance in that lifestyle. Unrepented sin gives the enemy an open door into your life to devour and destroy.

You may be thinking, "But Jesus defeated the Devil on Calvary." Christians often quote 1 John 3:8: "For this purpose the Son of God was manifested, that He might destroy the works of the devil." What are Satan's works? The word *works* is *ergon* in the Greek, which means "acts" or "deeds." We know through the Scriptures that Satan's works are to kill, steal, and destroy (John 10:10). We know that he also causes infirmities and sickness. For example, look at this passage:

> Now He was teaching in one of the synagogues on the Sabbath. And behold, there was a woman who had a spirit of infirmity eighteen years, and was bent over and could in no way raise herself up. But when Jesus saw her, He called her to Him and said to her, "Woman, you are loosed from your infirmity." And He laid His hands on her, and immediately she was made straight, and glorified God. But the ruler of the synagogue answered with indignation, because Jesus had healed on the Sabbath; and he said to the crowd, "There are six days on which men ought to work; therefore come and be healed on them, and not on the Sabbath day." The Lord then answered him and said, "Hypocrite! Does not each one of you on the Sabbath loose his ox or donkey from the stall, and lead it away to water it? So ought not this woman, being a daughter of Abraham, whom Satan has bound—think of it—for eighteen years, be loosed from this bond on the Sabbath? (Luke 13:10–16)

This woman whom Jesus recognized as being from the seed of Abraham and as an heir to the covenant had a crippling disease like severe curvature of the spine that had been caused by a spirit. Now, who had bound her with the infirmity? Satan. With His authority, Jesus loosed the infirmity, and immediately she was healed. The Greek word for *destroy* here means "to loosen" or "to break off."

First John 3:8 says this: "For this purpose the Son of God was manifested." Let's look at this purpose in its context.

> Whoever commits sin also commits lawlessness, and sin is lawlessness. And you know that He was manifested to take away our sins, and in Him there is no sin. Whoever abides in Him does not sin. Whoever sins has neither seen Him nor known Him. Little children, let no one deceive you. He who practices righteousness is righteous, just as He is righteous. He who sins is of the devil, for the devil has sinned from the beginning. For this purpose the Son of God was manifested, that He might destroy the works of the devil. Whoever has been born of God does not sin, for His seed remains in him; and he cannot sin, because he has been born of God." (1 John 3:4–9)

When we sin, we are not in position with Christ. Jesus was manifested to take away our sins (v. 5). He came to liberate us from the power of sin. Hallelujah! Now look at Romans 6:12–14: "Therefore do not let sin reign in your mortal body, that you should obey it in its lusts. And do not present your members as instruments of unrighteousness to sin, but present yourselves to God as being alive from the dead, and your members as instruments of righteousness to God. For sin shall not have dominion over you, for you are not under law but under grace." Jesus destroyed the power of sin over us, so now we are no longer slaves to sins, but slaves to righteousness (Romans 6:17–18).

Here is what the enemy doesn't want you to know: if we *position* ourselves in righteousness, he has no right in our lives. Some say that once we are made righteous (2 Corinthians 5:21), we stay righteous, no matter what. That's like saying once I took a bath, so now I will always be clean. No, I bathe daily to wash off the dirt I've picked up during the day. I am made righteous through Jesus Christ and His blood, but I must maintain my righteousness through forgiveness and repentance. That is the reason Satan is seeking whom he may devour. "Leave no [such] room or foothold for the devil [give no opportunity to him]" (Ephesians 4:27 AMP). Don't give the Devil a foothold or an opportunity in your life.

I know of no one who would want to give the Devil a foothold, knowing the consequences. So how do we prevent him from having this foothold? James 4:7 tells us to "submit to God. Resist the devil and he will flee from you." It is easy for most Christians to resist cancer or arthritis, but many have a hard time resisting the lusts of their flesh. Often that is because when they refuse to resist sin, they experience recurring sickness, missed opportunities, and financial troubles.

I love my wife's homemade brownies, but if I'm trying to diet, I don't karate chop them or throw them on the floor and stomp them. I simply use self-control and resist them. We resist the Devil the same way; we just put our hand in his face and say, "I resist you." When he tempts you to sin, just say no. Tell the Devil, "You can't touch me. I'm in position with God, and you'd have to go through Him to get to me, because I'm submitted to Him." When sickness tries to attack my body, that is what I confess. I also confess that my body is the temple of the living God, and it is strong enough to resist sickness and disease.

In Ephesians 6, Paul tells how we can equip ourselves to be invincible against the enemy: "Be strong in the Lord [be empowered through your union with Him]; draw your strength from Him [that strength which His boundless might provides]" (v. 10 AMP). We are to be strong in a particular position—that is, in the Lord through our union with Him. Our union with Him is the covenant we have with Him, which gives us His authority, His dominion, and His *dunamis* power over all powers of the enemy. To be strong in the Lord means in the Greek to be strengthened with *dunamis* (the same miracle-working power God anointed Jesus with; see Acts 10:38). "To be strengthened with" means that if I am in position with Him, I can do *all* things. "I can do all things through Christ who strengthens me" (Philippians 4:13).

It is the Holy Spirit living inside us that strengthens us. "He would grant you, according to the riches of His glory, to be strengthened with might through His Spirit in the inner man" (Ephesians 3:16).

When you are in position in Him and equipped with His armor, you will be able to stand against anything the enemy throws at you. So "put on the whole armor of God, that you may be able to stand against the wiles of the devil" (Ephesians 6:11). It is of uttermost importance that we put on and keep on all of the armor of God. Armor is heavy—Goliath's weighed more than 150 pounds. Some would like to leave certain pieces off—especially the breastplate of righteousness, which can be uncomfortable in wrong environments or friendships.

Wiles in the Greek is the word *methodeias*. It is where we get our word *method*. Satan has many methods, schemes, and plans to entrap, enslave, or defeat us. Another meaning is deceit or trickery. If he cannot deceive you by getting you to believe a lie, he has a hard time defeating you. He may try to tell you that you are not worthy, that you are going broke, that your marriage can't be fixed, that you can't be healed. Tell him what is written in the Word of God.

The armor of God gives you three abilities: the ability to stand against all enemies, the ability to withstand any and all attacks, and the ability to quench every fiery dart the enemy can throw at you.

Truth encircles you. Ephesians 6:14 says, "Stand therefore, having girded your waist with truth." One custom in biblical days was for the men to wear long, one-piece, flowing robes. When they were working, traveling, or in combat, they wore a wide belt made of either leather or metal. This belt would not only hold the robe in place, keeping it out of their way, but also gave them a place to attach their tools or weapons.

Isaiah 61:10 says, "I will greatly rejoice in the LORD, / My soul shall be joyful in my God; / For He has clothed me with the garments of salvation, / He has covered me with the robe of righteousness, / As a bridegroom decks himself with ornaments, / And as a bride adorns herself with her jewels." When we are born again, God covers us with robes of salvation and righteousness. Salvation doesn't merely mean being saved, getting our name written in the Lamb's Book of Life. *Salvation* in the Greek includes deliverance, preservation, prosperity, healing, happiness, and peace. Righteousness is being in right standing with God, in a place where God will protect, provide, and have intimacy with you. You can approach God and ask for your desires or ask for direction, knowing God will communicate with you.

These are all part of our covenant with God. As a child of God, you and I have a great inheritance—not when we get to heaven, but now. Satan would like to disrobe you of what is rightfully yours. But the only way the enemy can steal what is rightfully yours is the same way he stole from Adam: through deception. He got Eve to believe that what God said was not really the truth.

The Word of God is the highest truth there is; it supersedes any manmade philosophies, ideas, or what we consider to be truth. Hosea 4:6 says, "My people are destroyed for lack of knowledge." Many Christians are destroyed because they have no or little knowledge of the Word that will set them free, heal their bodies, deliver them from destruction, get them favor, and bring them blessings and prosperity. I believe that as we enter the last days, deception will very easily ensnare many believers. Those that position themselves in the complete truth will be hard to deceive. If you will get into the Word of God, you will find out who you are in Him, and find out what is rightfully yours because of what Jesus did on the cross. Then the enemy will have a difficult time deceiving you.

Put on the breastplate of righteousness. Ephesians 6:14 speaks of putting on the breastplate of righteousness. The breastplate (Greek *thorax*) was a piece of armor that covered the entire thoracic cavity, from the neck down to the thighs. It consisted of two parts; one covered the front, the other covered the back. It fastened together on the sides, which also provided protection. I cannot overemphasize the importance of staying positioned in *righteousness*. When we sin, we walk out from under God's provision of blessing and His protection.

Psalms 91 is often referred to as the protection chapter. Soldiers on the battlefield often armed themselves by reading and quoting it. Here are a few things mentioned in Psalm 91: God is our fortress and place of refuge. He will deliver us from the snares and arrows. We will not be afraid of the terror or destruction. A thousand may fall at our side, and ten thousand by our right foot, but it will not come close to us. No evil shall befall us and no plagues will come near our house. He will deliver us in times of trouble. These all belong to those that make God their dwelling place and place of refuge. When we stay in position, the enemy cannot touch us.

Be shod with the gospel. Ephesians 6:15 says, "And having shod your feet in preparation [to face the enemy with the firm-footed stability, the promptness, and the readiness produced by the good news] of the Gospel of peace" (AMP).

The gospel is the good news that Jesus preached: that we can experience the kingdom of heaven on earth and that God heals, forgives, and gives eternal life to those who trust Him. The Word of God is meant to give you a strong foundation, no matter what attack you face. God gives you assurance, confidence, and peace that if "He is for you who can be against you" (Romans 8:31).

Take the shield of faith. Ephesians 6:16 says, "Above all, taking the shield of faith with which you will be able to quench all the fiery darts of the wicked one." "Above all" does not mean that the shield of faith is at a higher level than the rest of the armor. It is two Greek words—*en pasin*—that mean "to go in front of." Faith is not meant to follow you or go beside you; it is meant to go before you to stop the Devil and all his weapons before they reach you. A combat soldier's shield looked more like a door than a trash-can lid. Those small, circular ones were often decorated and embossed with gold and silver and used for parades. When a soldier enlisted in the army, he was measured, and a shield was made to fit his height. It covered him from the ground to the top of his head. The enemy will easily give up to those who are positioned with the shield of faith.

Wear the helmet of salvation. Ephesians 6:17 says, "And take the helmet of salvation." Soldiers wore helmets to protect their heads. We are three-part beings. We are spirit—the eternal part that never ceases to exist; we have a physical body; and we have a soul. Our soul, like our spirit, cannot be seen. The soul consists of our mind, our will, and our emotions. These are mostly based in our brains, where a mortal blow would cause death; therefore, soldiers wore their helmets during battle.

From our minds, visions are created. God gives us visions of life, prosperity, the future, and hope (Jeremiah 29:11). Satan, on the other hand, wants to give us visions of dying, destitution, sickness, and hopelessness. Through your emotions, the enemy would like to bind you with a spirit of fear. Many Christians live in fear, which works just like faith: it is an expectation and anticipation. However, it focuses on something bad happening. But God has given us faith and hope.

2 Timothy 1:7 says, "For God has not given us a spirit of fear, but of power and of love and of a sound mind." The helmet of salvation

is to keep the enemy from programming our minds and emotions with fear and defeat.

> For though we walk (live) in the flesh, we are not carrying on our warfare according to the flesh and using mere human weapons. For the weapons of our warfare are not physical [weapons of flesh and blood], but they are mighty before God for the overthrow and destruction of strongholds, [Inasmuch as we] refute arguments and theories and reasonings and every proud and lofty thing that sets itself up against the [true] knowledge of God; and we lead every thought and purpose away captive into the obedience of Christ (the Messiah, the Anointed One). (2 Corinthians 10:3–5 AMP)

Remember, Scripture tells we are to put on the whole armor of God. That armor is meant to protect us from any and all attacks of the enemy. But you must not only put on every piece of it, you must keep it on. If the enemy sees your shield go down, he will attack you with fear and doubt. If he sees your breastplate missing, he will get you into sin and out of relationship with God and His protection. If he can get you to drop your belt of truth, he will fill you with doubt and unbelief. We must stay in our armor, in position at all times.

We've been focusing on the defensive side of our warfare. Now let's look at our offensive weapons, which are mighty.

The sword of the Spirit. Ephesians 6:17 says, "And take the sword of the Spirit, which is the word of God." The reason Paul lists the armor first is that weapons are useless if you are not in position with the armor. No matter how sharp the sword is, it has no effect if truth, faith, and righteousness are not there to back it up. The sword of the Spirit, which is the Word of God, is not a formula that we can merely speak. It must be declared out of believing the truth; it must be proclaimed with authority by those who are positioned in righteousness and established in faith.

Jesus, who was fully equipped, defeated Satan by declaring what was written. He overrode every temptation Satan had by being positioned with God's authority. For the sword to be effective, you must study it, meditate on it, memorize it, quote it, and most of all, believe it.

Prayer. Ephesians 6:18 say that we are to "[pray] always with all prayer and supplication in the Spirit." For soldiers to be effective in battle, they must be in communication with their commanding officer, who has all the strategies for the battle. We are to use all types of prayer to defeat the enemy. One of the most powerful is praying the Word out loud. When I'm in a battle with sickness, I speak the healing Scriptures from my mouth with a voice of authority. When I'm under financial attack, I pray out loud, reminding the enemy that I tithe and that God will rebuke him, the devourer. We need to always pray the prayer of faith (James 5:15). In fact, all our prayers should be in faith, or we shouldn't expect an answer.

The prayer of binding and loosing is a very effective weapon against the enemy. Lou Ann keeps a written prayer in her Bible into which she inserts the names of people who are in bondage to the enemy. Calling out their names, she binds their minds, wills, and emotions to the mind, will, and emotions of Jesus Christ. She binds their feet to paths of righteousness. She looses every ungodly, unmoral, and unrighteous relationship from them, and looses addiction or sin from them in order to free them. The Greek word for *bind* means "to adhere" or "to tie up." To loose means to release, crush, or destroy.

In Scripture, keys are symbols of authority. Prayers of binding and loosing are prayers that release authority. As a child of God, Jesus gives you those keys. He says, "And I will give you the keys of the kingdom of heaven, and whatever you bind on earth will be bound in heaven, and whatever you loose on earth will be loosed in heaven" (Matthew 16:19).

There also is the prayer of agreement, when you set yourself in agreement in faith with another believer. Jesus said, "Again I say to you that if two of you agree on earth concerning anything that they ask, it will be done for them by My Father in heaven. For where two or three are gathered together in My name, I am there in the midst of them" (Matthew 16:19–20). One of the most powerful types of prayer we can pray is in the Spirit or in a prayer language. Romans 8:26–27 says, "So too the [Holy] Spirit comes to our aid and bears us up in our weakness; for we do not know what prayer to offer nor how to offer it worthily as we ought, but the Spirit Himself goes to meet our supplication and pleads in our behalf with unspeakable yearnings and groanings too deep for utterance. And He Who searches the hearts of men knows what is in the mind of the [Holy] Spirit [what His intent is], because the Spirit intercedes and pleads [before God] in behalf of the saints according to and in harmony with God's will" (AMP).

There are times we feel an urgency to pray and do not know what, how, or for whom to pray. The Holy Spirit inside you knows. Here is one of the best examples I know of: Back in the eighties, Lou Ann and I hosted a Bible study for some cowboys and cowgirls attending West Texas State University. They had all received the baptism of the Holy Spirit with the gift of praying in an unknown tongue. One of the couples was sitting down to eat lunch one day. As Bobby began to bless the meal, he suddenly began to pray in the Spirit. Shortly after he prayed, they received a phone call from his mother. She asked if they saw the news on TV. Then she went on to give details of an incident that happened in their hometown.

Bobby's father, a deputy sheriff, was patrolling a rural road when he noticed a parked car. He pulled up beside it, rolled down his window, and asked the driver if he was okay. The man inside the car raised a double-barreled sawed off shotgun and fired both barrels point-blank toward Bobby's dad. The blasts blew out the back window and the windshield of the patrol car, but not one pellet touched his dad. Bobby asked his mom what time that happened, and it was the very same moment that he switched from blessing the food to praying in the Holy Spirit.

Friend, if you are not baptized in the Holy Ghost, evidenced by speaking in tongues, you need to ask God to baptize you now. You will receive power like the disciples experienced in the book of Acts. It will strengthen your faith. Jude 1:20 says, "But you, beloved, build yourselves up [founded] on your most holy faith [make progress, rise like an edifice higher and higher], praying in the Holy Spirit" (AMP).

As a soldier in God's magnificent overcoming army, position yourself to win the battle.

Chapter 12

POSITIONED TO RELEASE THE ANOINTING

> For we are to God the fragrance of Christ among
> those who are being saved and among those who
> are perishing. To the one we are the aroma of death
> leading to death, and to the other the aroma of life
> leading to life. And who is sufficient for these things?
> 2 Corinthians 2:15–16

Several years ago a mouse or some other kind of varmint died in the wall of our house. We sprayed aromatic fragrances and burned candles, which masked the horrendous odor for a few hours. Finally we found a product that absorbed the smell, and within a few days, no one could detect the smell of the decomposing body entombed in our bedroom wall.

Imagine someone inventing a fragrant mist that completely changes the atmosphere in which it was released. This product is so powerful that it can even change situations and circumstances. With this product, you can walk the halls of local hospitals, spraying all the occupants that lie in the beds. As soon as the mist touches their bodies, health and healing immediately overtake them. Cancer cells shrivel up and die; deadly viruses disappear; eyes that were blinded by chemicals begin to see clearly; ears devastated by the blast of a bomb suddenly begin to hear voices praising and thanking God.

The holder of this mystical spray can go to the elevator and push the button to the next floor, where patients are locked behind doors and security personnel pace the hall. This floor is filled with the screams of those in torment as they are detoxing from the cocaine and heroin, meth, and alcohol. Others are strapped to their bed to keep them from wounding themselves. Their wrists are bandaged to hide the wounds from suicide attempts. Some are in a comatose condition, concealing depression.

As these occupants are sprayed, the atmosphere changes. An awareness of peace enters, and even the foul smell leaves. All of a sudden, like the fans at a playoff football game whose team has just scored the winning touchdown, the occupants begin to shout, "I'm finally free! I'm finally free!"

There *is* something that can be released to change situations, restore health to the sick, and release the captives. It is the anointing of God. Following Jesus' temptation in the wilderness, He goes to the temple in Nazareth and makes the following proclamation:

> "The Spirit of the LORD is upon Me,
> Because He has anointed Me to preach the gospel to the poor;
> He has sent Me
> To heal the brokenhearted,
> To proclaim liberty to the captives
> And recovery of sight to the blind,
> To set at liberty those who are oppressed;
> To proclaim the acceptable year of the LORD." (Luke 4:18–19)

The word *anoint* comes from the Hebrew word *mashach,* which means to rub or smear, usually with oil. Anointing is symbolic for setting

121

someone apart for a specific purpose. Today we anoint those that are called into the ministry, or the office of elder, or deacon in order to recognize their call and purpose. The trouble is, today we don't recognize the true anointing. We hear someone with a beautiful voice and we say, "What an anointed singer she is!" Or we hear someone with great oratorical skills and we say, "What an anointed preacher he is!" We often confuse talent with anointing. Talent entertains us; anointing empowers us to release the supernatural.

Jesus was saying that God had anointed Him to preach, to heal, to deliver, and to release. Whom God anoints, He empowers. The anointing is like the wind; you cannot see it, but you can see its results. Prophetically speaking, Isaiah says, "The yoke will be destroyed because of the anointing" (10:17). The anointing is God's incarnate power on man. Remember, God made Jesus to be flesh and blood just like you and me, but Jesus was able to stay in position with God to release God's power through the anointing. Acts 10:38 says, "God anointed Jesus of Nazareth with the Holy Spirit and with power, who went about doing good and healing all who were oppressed by the devil, for God was with Him." You want to talk about something that has 100 percent results? It was the anointing of God on Jesus. Everybody He ministered to got healed and delivered. Jesus wasn't selective; He healed *all* because He knew this was the will of His Father God.

Wouldn't it be nice if people today could release the anointing? Well, the disciples did, and if you will position yourself in Christ, you can also. You cannot get the anointing through education, you cannot get it because you reach a certain age, and you cannot earn it because of what you've done. You receive it because God wants to release heaven onto earth, and if you will simply position yourself, you can have His anointing also. I love the following account.

Now Peter and John went up together to the temple at the hour of prayer, the ninth hour. And a certain man lame from his mother's womb was carried, whom they laid daily at the gate of the temple which is called Beautiful, to ask alms from those who entered the temple; who, seeing Peter and John about to go into the temple, asked for alms. And fixing his eyes on him, with John, Peter said, "Look at us." So he gave them his attention, expecting to receive something from them. Then Peter said, "Silver and gold I do not have, but what I do have I give you: In the name of Jesus Christ of Nazareth, rise up and walk." And he took him by the right hand and lifted him up, and immediately his feet and ankle bones received strength. So he, leaping up, stood and walked and entered the temple with them—walking, leaping, and praising God. And all the people saw him walking and praising God. Then they knew that it was he who sat begging alms at the Beautiful Gate of the temple; and they were filled with wonder and amazement at what had happened to him. (Acts 3:1–10)

I can just see and hear Peter and John. They had experienced what Jesus had said would occur: if they would pray, believe, and expect, He would release the anointing He had into their lives. The anointing was not downsized, but the very same power that God had anointed Jesus with to heal the sick and deliver the captives. Jesus said, "Do you not believe that I am in the Father, and the Father in Me? The words that I speak to you I do not speak on My own authority; but the Father who dwells in Me does the works. Believe Me that I am in the Father and the Father in Me, or else believe Me for the sake of the works themselves. Most assuredly, I say to you, he who believes in Me, the works that I do he will do also; and greater works than these he will do, because I go to My Father" (John 14:10–12). He is saying that when He goes back to the Father, the Father would release

His anointing onto His followers. And they would not only do the same works of miracles that Jesus did, but *greater* works.

Peter and John had just received the power of the Holy Spirit, and I believe they were looking for someone to release God's power on. One might think they would say, "Let's find something easy like someone with a headache." But no, God had something that looked impossible to them: a forty-year-old man that had never walked. He was born a cripple *not* because it was God's will or God's judgment. But, it was God's perfect will to heal him. When a person releases the anointing in faith, three things happen: the supernatural will overcome the natural; God will be glorified; and it will cause others to praise God.

Listen to what Peter boldly says to him: "Silver and gold I do not have, but what I do have I give you: In the name of Jesus Christ of Nazareth, rise up and walk" (Acts 3:6). Peter told him that he could give him what he had. You cannot give something you don't have. Many believers try to give something they don't have. "Well," you might say, "I thought signs and wonders are to follow all who believe." Yes, that should be the *norm* for all believers. If we are in covenant with God, we should be leaving behind us a trail of healed and delivered people. The trouble is, it is not happening very much. Some Christians aren't releasing any anointing because they simply believe they don't have any. But if you have the Holy Spirit in you, you have an anointing (1 John 2:20). The same power that Jesus released to the blind, the sick, the deaf, the demon possessed, and the dead resides in you, but you must be in and stay in position to release it.

When we think of the word *have*, we usually think of possessing something. Peter wasn't saying that he possessed something special. If it were something special, men would want to praise Peter. Here the word for *have* is the Greek word *hyparcho,* which is actually two words joined to means "under rule." Peter was releasing the Father's authority, whom he represented. *No one can release authority unless he or she is submitted to authority.* Being under God's authority means that we are submitted to all His word, not just the words we want to submit to. Many Christians are good at quoting the promises of God, but they do not receive them because they refuse to submit to His authority. For example, the blessings found in Deuteronomy 28 are meant for all believers, but only if they submit to obeying the voice of God. Disobeying the scriptural laws of tithing often keeps Christians from releasing the anointing. Any unrepented sin also will stop the anointing. Failing to submit to the authority that God places in the church will also stop the anointing.

Jesus released the power of God without fail, because He was submitted to authority. Look at this account about a man on death's bed in Matthew 8.

> Now when Jesus had entered Capernaum, a centurion came to Him, pleading with Him, saying, "Lord, my servant is lying at home paralyzed, dreadfully tormented." And Jesus said to him, "I will come and heal him." The centurion answered and said, "Lord, I am not worthy that You should come under my roof. But only speak a word, and my servant will be healed. For I also am a man under authority, having soldiers under me. And I say to this one, 'Go,' and he goes; and to another, 'Come,' and he comes; and to my servant, 'Do this,' and he does it." When Jesus heard it, He marveled, and said to those who followed, "Assuredly, I say to you, I have not found such great faith, not even in Israel!"

Continuing on, you will see that his servant was healed as soon as Jesus said he was healed. This soldier was a man of means who had his own servant, and he evidently commanded a battalion of soldiers.

He had the authority to send his soldiers wherever they were needed, as long as he stayed under authority of the officer over him. If he had failed to submit to that officer, his authority over his men would have ceased to exist. By revelation, maybe from listening to or observing Jesus, he recognized that Jesus was also under a higher authority. He recognized that when Jesus spoke, His words exercised authority over sickness, disease, and demons. Jesus was totally submitted to His Father. He never committed sin, which tells you how submitted He was to His Father's authority. He said only what He heard His Father saying, and He did only what He saw His Father doing (Matthew 8:5–10).

We tend to try to do what we see others do. We see a pastor or evangelist lay hands on someone and that person gets healed, so we try it—and nothing happens. Maybe in time or through medicine, that person's health is restored, but nothing supernatural happens. We might even try to cast out a spirit of addiction from someone, but to no avail. Our faith begins to weaken, and we become discouraged, thinking, *we just don't have the anointing.*

Some men who saw the miracles that were happening with the disciples thought it was pretty cool, so they tried it with no success. Here's what happened:

> Some of the itinerant Jewish exorcists took it upon themselves to call the name of the Lord Jesus over those who had evil spirits, saying, "We exorcise you by the Jesus whom Paul preaches." Also there were seven sons of Sceva, a Jewish chief priest, who did so. And the evil spirit answered and said, "Jesus I know, and Paul I know; but who are you?" Then the man in whom the evil spirit was leaped on them, overpowered them, and prevailed against them, so that they fled out of that house naked and wounded." (Acts 19:13–16)

Did you notice they were itinerant Jews (covenant), meaning they weren't connected? Often we see people wanting a ministry, but they do not want to be submitted to a church. It is good to place yourself under someone who is submitted to authority in order to be mentored in praying for the sick and casting out demons, but don't try to copy someone without being totally submitted to God's authority.

Peter was successful because he was operating under authority given to him. Authority must be given; it cannot be taken. Taking your own authority is called rebellion. Jesus was delegated *all authority in Heaven and all authority on earth* (Matthew 28:18) Jesus delegated His authority to His disciples. A disciple is not only referring to those that served with Jesus, but refers to all who follow, put their trust in and adhere to his words. (John 8:31) Therefore, if you and I position ourselves in Him and His words are positioned in our lives, then we are His disciples. "And when he called His twelve disciples to Him, He gave them power over uncleaned spirits to cast them out, and to heal all kinds of sickness and all kinds of disease" (Matthew 10:1). Chapters and verses were put into the Bible for our convenience of finding Scriptures, but you do not begin a chapter with *and*. Read Matthew 9:35–38 for a better understanding of this verse. Jesus had been healing every sickness and disease among the people. When He saw the multitudes sick and bound up, it was very emotional to Him. He compared it to a great harvest, that in the natural He needed some help, so he *released power* into them through His authority, and then He commissioned them to go release it: "And as you go, preach, saying, 'The kingdom of heaven is at hand.' Heal the sick, cleanse the lepers, raise the dead, and cast out demons. Freely you have received, freely give" (Matthew 10:7–8).

The word *commission* means "authority to perform a task." As a child of God, you have been commissioned into this world. "And He said to them, 'Go into all the world and preach the gospel to every creature. He who believes and is baptized will be saved; but he who does not believe will be condemned. And these signs will follow those who believe: In My name they will cast out demons; they will speak with new tongues; they will take up serpents; and if they drink anything deadly, it will by no means hurt them; they will lay hands on the sick, and they will recover" (Mark 16:15–18).

James 4:7 says that when you submit to God—His voice, His Word—the devil must flee. You have an assignment from the Most High God, and He has equipped you to do the task, but you must submit to all of His authority. When we position our lives by yielding to Him, this positions us so that His anointing will flow through us.

We are seeing countless people healed through words of knowledge without even praying for them, because the word from God carries the anointing, and when it is embraced, it immediately breaks the yoke. Recently I said during a midweek service that I believed we were entering a season when the anointing of God would heal people just sitting under the Word. That way they could not say, Well, so-and-so prayed, laid hands on me, and I was healed." God doesn't share His glory with us; we only get to see it.

After the service, I was visiting with a couple of men when a woman walked up to me and said, "I want to shake your hand." I stretched out my hand, and she squeezed it like an arm wrestler. I thought, *What is she trying to prove?* When she finished her display of strength, she said, "I came into the service awaiting surgery for a broken wrist. My wrist was in extreme pain; I could not move it or my fingers. As soon as you spoke those words about healing, the pain left. I removed my cast." Then she pulled the cast from her purse. Friend, the anointing of God is not only for every believer to operate in, but God expects that we will use it to free the captives.

Chapter 13

POSITIONED FOR SONSHIP

I do not want to appear to be a male chauvinist to all the females reading this, but sons are very important. I am highly blessed to have three beautiful daughters, Steph, Brooke, and Brandi that both love God and serve God. All three are married to godly men who are like sons to me. All three have given my wife and me the grandest things: grandkids. I always expected that when the time came, I would have sons. In fact, I prayed, believed, and confessed that I would have sons. We even decorated the nursery for little boys and bought boy clothes, but to my surprise, we had girls. Rooms had to be redecorated and clothes returned, and I became surrounded by girls. It's like the old song by Maurice Chevalier, "Thank Heaven for Little Girls." I thank God, who in His infinite wisdom destined me to be a dad to daughters. I would not have had it any different. I love my daughters.

I was born in a little West Texas town during World War II. My mother was a teenage girl living at home with her parents. My dad, a naval pilot, was stationed on an aircraft carrier in the South Pacific. In those days, sonograms had not been invented, so a child's gender could not be determined until he or she made an entrance into this world. Communication to spouses in the service was limited to letters and telegraphs. My dad anxiously waited for the letter announcing the birth of his son. Dad said he was overjoyed to see he had a son to carry on the Jones family name. It was very special to him, since all of his siblings were girls. My granddad was a farmer/rancher who had three daughters and had always longed for a little boy to follow in his footsteps. Though my mother's two sisters were married, they had not given birth, so I was not only the first grandchild but also the first grandson.

Throughout history, God had never had a son. The human race had begun with Adam, whom God formed from the dust of the earth and then breathed into that he might become a living being. Then God realized that man needed a companion, so out of Adam he brought a woman to fulfill him. Through this union, the human race began with their offspring, Cain and Abel. One can see how fast man multiplied through Noah and others. God had this human race that would carry out His will on earth, and God would fellowship with them. In one sense, Adam was a created son. When man sinned, this allowed the enemy to wreak havoc, death and destruction on planet Earth. But God had a plan. This time He would not create another son, but he would "birth" His Son.

When the time was right, God chose a young, virgin Jewish girl, who would carry and nurture His seed. Here is the story:

> Then the angel told her: Do not be afraid, Mary, for you have found favor with God. Now listen: You will conceive and give birth to a son, and you will call His name Jesus. He will be great and will be called the Son of the Most High, and the Lord God will give Him the throne of His father David. He will reign over the house of Jacob forever, and His kingdom will have no end. Mary asked the angel, "How can this be, since I have not been intimate with a man?" The angel replied to her: "The Holy Spirit will come upon you, and the power of

the Most High will overshadow you. Therefore, the holy One to be born will be called the Son of God." (Luke 1:30–34 HCSB)

God implanted the seed of His holy, sinless child within the womb of Mary. This Child was to be born of a woman, but carry the DNA of His Father, God. The Word who was with God from the beginning and was God became God in a human form. "And the Word became flesh and dwelt among us, and we beheld His glory, the glory as of the only begotten of the Father, full of grace and truth" (John 1:14–15).

One of the most familiar passages in the Bible tell us that Jesus was the "only begotten" Son, whom God sent because He so loved the world, He sacrificed Him to redeem us from eternal damnation. (John 3:16) The Greek word for *only* means that Jesus was the *only* one of a race, family, or kind. He was all God in power and authority, yet He was in the form of man. This *super being* came to restore authority and dominion over planet Earth to mankind.

Jesus also came to destroy all of Satan's evil works and plans toward mankind. Sickness, disease, mental illnesses, infirmities, bondage of sin, and every evil work could not stay in place when His anointing was present. "How God anointed and consecrated Jesus of Nazareth with the [Holy] Spirit and with strength and ability and power; how He went about doing good and, in particular, curing all who were harassed and oppressed by [the power of] the devil, for God was with Him" (Acts 10:38 AMP). And 1 John 3:8 says, "The reason the Son of God was made manifest (visible) was to undo (destroy, loosen, and dissolve) the works the devil [has done]" (AMP). These two verses clarify God's purpose for birthing His Son. His power through His Son had no limits; *nothing was impossible. All* the sick were healed, *all* the lame walked, *all* the blind saw, and *all* that died prematurely were raised from the dead. His authority released the oppressed, those in bondage. It stopped the wind and calmed the seas. It created, it multiplied, and there were *no limits* on the Son of God.

Becoming members of this divine race is one of the great privileges you have. Through faith, you can become children of God by realizing and acknowledging you are a sinner. Then by faith, ask Him to come into your life. John 1:12 says, "But to as many as did receive and welcome Him, He gave the authority (power, privilege, right) to become the children of God, that is, to those who believe in (adhere to, trust in, and rely on) His name" (AMP).

The often-used phrase "come into my life" can be confusing, unless we understand our makeup. We are created in the likeness of God, who is eternal and triune in being. We are made of a body that houses our unseen soul (mind, will, and emotions) and a spirit. Our spirit is eternal. If not reborn, it will spend eternity in hell; if reborn, in heaven. Jesus told Nicodemus that if he wanted eternal life he must be born-again. How can you and I become born-again? The "seed of God" must impregnate our spirit. As 1 Peter 1:23 says, "You have been regenerated (born again), not from a mortal origin (seed, sperm), but from one that is immortal by the ever living and lasting Word of God" (AMP).

When we receive Jesus Christ by believing, embracing, and trusting Him as our Lord and Savior, our spirit conceives His nature and we become a new creation. We become children in the family of God. It is a privilege and great honor to be called and considered a child of God. The Greek word for *child* or *children* is *technon*. Babies have no responsibility, they are just loved, nurtured, and taken care of by their parents, but as they become toddlers, they begin to have some accountability. There are things they cannot do. They are not to touch certain things; if they do so, they are punished.

I like it when parents put perimeters around their toddlers using voice commands instead of putting things out of reach. This teaches them responsibility and the consequences for their actions. Children have very limited authority because of their maturity. You can't give a child a loaded gun or keys to your car, because they will probably hurt themselves or others. You can't give them your credit card and send them to town, because they would not make wise decisions. As they grow in maturity, you begin to release more authority to them.

Even though Jesus was God in the flesh, He didn't exercise His authority as a child or youth. It is not recorded in the Bible that He performed any miracles until His adulthood. When Jesus reached adulthood, "John bore witness, saying, 'I saw the Spirit descending from heaven like a dove, and He remained upon Him. I did not know Him, but He who sent me to baptize with water said to me, "Upon whom you see the Spirit descending, and remaining on Him, this is He who baptizes with the Holy Spirit" And I have seen and testified that this is the Son of God" (John 1:32).

Matthew 3:17 says that a voice from heaven said, "This is my beloved Son, in whom I am well pleased." God is not a male chauvinist, and neither am I, and "son" in the Greek refers not to *gender* but to *maturity.* A son is one who represents His father with authority. From this point on in Jesus' ministry, we see where He began to flow in the supernatural. Many of His children have remained children because they have never walked in accountability, submission, and obedience. They have been touched by the Holy Spirit, but their childlike immaturity has not allowed the Holy Spirit to *remain* on them.

I am not taking away from the deity of Jesus Christ. He is God revealed to man; there is no other, just as there is no other God. He is the way, the truth, and the life, and no one comes to the Father except through Him. (John 14:6) We worship Him as the *Son* of God. At one time He was the *only* Son of God, but now God has many sons. Romans 8:29 says, "For whom He foreknew, He also predestined to be conformed to the image of His Son, that He might be the firstborn among many brethren." *Brethren* means offspring from the same womb or parents. Jesus was the first Son of many sons. Firstborn sons had special privileges and rights. God has highly exalted Him and given Him the name which is *above* every name" (Philippians 2:9).

The world is waiting for sons of God. Romans 8:19 says, "For [even the whole] creation (all nature) waits expectantly and longs earnestly for God's sons to be made known [waits for the revealing, the disclosing of their sonship]" (AMP). All of God's creation is waiting for sons to restore order and to bring God's will in heaven to planet Earth and all its inhabitants. For sons to bring healing and deliverance to mankind. For sons to take authority over all the works of their adversary, the Devil.

I love the word for *adopt* in the Greek (*huithesia*). It means "to place as a son". *To place* means to put into position. One is put into position as a son through adoption. According to Romans 8:15, "For you did not receive the spirit of bondage again to fear, but you received the Spirit of adoption by whom we cry out, 'Abba, Father.'" In some cultures, it was very important for a father to have a son to carry on his family name and to be an heir of the father's wealth.

Adoption releases us. In the natural, when a child is adopted, the birth parents relinquish all right to the child. They can't say where he goes to school, what kind of clothes he can wear, or what he eats. In fact they do not have any right for visitation unless the adoptive parents agree. When you were adopted into the family of God, all of your past obligations and debts were canceled. You got a fresh start and a new beginning. The Devil no longer has any rights in your life; in fact, he has even lost visitation rights. The only way he can now visit you is by your allowing him to. Adoption releases you to become a son with a new Father.

Adoption positions us as sons. Law considers adoptees legal children. Adoption is the act by which God gives His born-again children an adult standing in the family. The adopted son of God has all the rights of a legitimate son; in fact, he is considered a legal child.

Adoption as a son entitles you to your inheritance. Galatians 4:1–7 says,

> Now I say that the heir, as long as he is a child, does not differ at all from a slave, though he is master of all, but is under guardians and stewards until the time appointed by the father. Even so we, when we were children, were in bondage under the elements of the world. But when the fullness of the time had come, God sent forth His Son, born of a woman, born under the law, to redeem those who were under the law, that we might receive the adoption as sons. And because you are sons, God has sent forth the Spirit of His Son into your hearts, crying out, "Abba, Father!" Therefore you are no longer a slave but a son, and if a son, then an heir of God through Christ.

Even though children in the natural and children in the Kingdom of God have an inheritance, it is the Father's wisdom not to release it to them until they are mature enough to handle it. God may have the call to preach or pastor on one's life, He will not release the gift until they are mature enough to handle it. He may have the gifts of healings and miracles in another, but if they received it as a child, it would go to their heads and they would probably become prideful. Sonship and maturity releases the gift into our lives.

Throughout church history we have seen and heard of great men and women of God whom God used to bring revival, to miraculously heal the sick, to cast out demons, and even to raise the dead. It is not that God loved them any more or favored them any more, or gave them a greater anointing. The power of God is available to all, but all do not release the power of God. This is due to the fact that they learned to position themselves so the power of God could flow through them.

Children are easily distracted. Mature sons are focused. No matter what was going around Him, Jesus never lost His focus on His Father. He was always aware of what His Father desired to say or do. If we are going to become mature sons, our focus must be on Him. No matter where we are, we must have an awareness of what He wants to do through us and, what He wants to say through us.

Christians tend to place themselves in this position when they are in the house of God or with other believers. Jesus was so focused on His Father that even when He was in the cities with all the commotion going on He knew what His Father was doing, and He imparted it to others. God wants His sons to have the same awareness of Him, so that no matter where we are—if we are at the supermarkets or at a ballgame—when we hear His voice, we respond and impart that word of knowledge or wisdom that will bring life or answers to someone who is struggling. When we have an awareness of what He is doing, we will boldly go up to those who He directs us to and impart His healing anointing into their bodies.

Romans 8:14 gives us the criteria for becoming a son: "For all who are led by the Spirit of God are sons of God" (AMP). The verb *led* does not mean to be dragged or coerced; it involves a willingness to follow. Sons are so hungry for their Father that they desire to be in His presence continually. They understand that they must bow down in their hearts in complete submission to Him. We cannot follow Him and satisfy our fleshly desires by continuing in sin. Sons are not led by fact. Sons are not led by emotions. When Sons are led by the Spirit of God that lives inside them, then the signs, wonders, and miracles will follow.

John 1:12 says, "But as many as received Him, to them He gave the right to become children of God, to those who believe in His name." From their birth, my children had the right to be my children. They had a birthright, but that birthright did not give them authority to use my credit cards or my checking account. However, when they became of age and I saw maturity in them, I allowed them use of my credit cards. The word *right* here does not mean privilege. It is the Greek word *exousia*, which means "authority." When you and I adhere to His name—that is, the authority of who He is as the begotten Son of God—He empowers us to become sons of God. Because we are His representatives on Earth, He gives us the authority to release His will that is in heaven onto the inhabitants of earth. Now John 14:12 becomes a reality to us: "Most assuredly, I say to you, he who believes in Me, the works that I do he will do also; and greater works than these he will do, because I go to My Father. And whatever you ask in My name, that I will do, that the Father may be glorified in the Son."

There are children around the world living in orphanages, waiting for someone to pick them for adoption. No matter where you were born, what race or color you are, before the foundation of this earth God planned for you to become one of His sons—a son He could empower to heal the sick, deliver the captives, and raise the dead, a son He could release His power and authority through. As Ephesians 1:3–6 says,

> Blessed be the God and Father of our Lord Jesus Christ, who has blessed us with every spiritual blessing in the heavenly places in Christ, just as He chose us in Him

before the foundation of the world, that we should be holy and without blame before Him in love, having predestined us to adoption as sons by Jesus Christ to Himself, according to the good pleasure of His will, to the praise of the glory of His grace, by which He has made us accepted in the Beloved.

Chapter 14

POSITIONED FOR INTIMACY WITH GOD

I met Lou Ann on a blind date October 31, 1976. I moved to Austin, Texas, after becoming a Christian and began attending a dynamic Baptist church, where Larry, an old college schoolmate, and his wife were leaders of the young marrieds. Larry and I had nothing in common in college, he played basketball and I rodeoed. *Jocks* and *cowboys* didn't mix or hang out together. We only knew each other by recognition at that time. Though we were acquainted by name only in college, because of our relationship with Christ, our friendship flourished at the church. We played golf and shared meals regularly.

Larry and Joyce believed it was their mission in life to be a matchmaker for me. Larry was a representative for a company that called on dentists in the Austin area. While golfing one day, Larry began telling me of a girl who worked for one of his dental clients. He wrote her name and phone number on one of his business cards and exhorted me to ask her out. Not being big on blind dates, I ignored his request, but for some reason I put the card with her name and phone number on my visor. Larry had also been working the other side of the fence with Lou Ann. He had been telling her about his friend, a cowboy and former bull rider who had become a Christian.

She let him know very quickly that she was definitely not interested in cowboys, much less a bull rider.

Larry was very persistent with me; each time we were together, he would ask, "Have you called Lou Ann yet?" Finally, being dateless one week, I gave in and called her and she agreed to a date. When she opened the door, I saw that she was even more attractive than Larry had described.

During dinner I found out that her dad was a rancher and that she was from San Angelo, Texas. I told her I was going to a roping in San Angelo in a couple of weeks and asked if she would like to go with me. We went to church the following Sunday, and afterward she said she would love to go and see her family and also go to the roping with me.

I had been asking God for several months for a wife; in fact, I had told him exactly everything I wanted in a wife. Even though we had just met and had dated only a few times, I felt like Lou Ann was the one for me, so driving back to Austin I popped the question and asked her to marry me. A few days later, she answered yes and on January 10, 2013, we celebrated thirty-seven years of enraptured marriage. Even though we dated only a couple of months before getting married, I knew Lou Ann, but yet I really didn't know her. It has taken time, but we have become so intimate with each other that we have truly become one flesh.

God has always desired an intimate relationship with mankind; in fact, that is why He created man in His likeness so that He could have a personal relationship with us. Adam and Eve enjoyed total intimacy with God, until sin erected a wall between them and Him. God so desired to restore that intimacy with mankind that he literally became one of us. Jesus Christ became flesh, and through His death and resurrection, we can become intimate with the God of creation.

In Philippians 3:8–10, Paul says, "I also count all things loss … that I may know Him and the power of His resurrection." Do I mean the apostle Paul, the one that had such a dramatic God encounter on the road to Damascus, the one that was jailed and beaten for his faith in Jesus Christ, the one that performed many miracles in His name, the one who birthed churches and wrote two-thirds of the New Testament? Why did he say that he wanted to know Him? The word *know* here means to be intimate with. It is beyond having knowledge of someone or recognizing who someone is.

I love how the Amplified version says it: "[For my determined purpose is] that I may know Him [that I may progressively become more deeply and intimately acquainted with Him, perceiving and recognizing and understanding the wonders of His Person more strongly and more clearly]." This is how our relationship with Jesus should go; we meet Him and then we progressively become more deeply and intimately acquainted with Him. That is how Lou Ann's relationship and mine has evolved. We met and were attracted to one another, continued to see one another, fell in love, and entered into the covenant of marriage. Our relationship doesn't end there; because of our love for one another and our commitment to each other, we are never satisfied with yesterday's intimacy, but rather desire to become closer to each other every new day we share.

If your desire is to just become acquainted with Him, you might make it to heaven. But if you are determined to become deeply and intimately acquainted with Him, perceiving and recognizing the wonders of His purpose, then hang on; you are in for a great adventure. The more intimate with Him you become, the more your relationship will be like the covenant of marriage. You will become as one flesh with Him as He leads you into your destiny. Knowing Him in this manner will begin to release the powers of who He is into your life, and you will become an extension of Him on this earth.

In our fast-paced, microwaveable world, we develop very few intimate relationships, even with family members. However, we all have multitudes of acquaintances. They may include the checker at our local grocery store, a neighbor, or a church member. We have facial recognition of them, and we probably know their names and may even drop their names in our conversations. But truthfully we know very little about them; we are just acquainted with them.

Many are just acquainted with Him. They know who He is, why He came, and why He died. From time to time His name comes up in their conversations, and most of them have probably cried out to Him when they needed help. They know Him as one knows a movie star, a famous singer, or the president. They recognize Him, but have never met Him. Others have met Him, put their faith in Him, loved Him, but have never really become intimate with Him. We've all met someone that we instantly liked, and we thought our relationship would develop into a close and deep one. But years later we may meet for lunch, exchange Christmas cards, or have occasional long conversations, but that deep friendship never materialized. Sadly, many Christians have had a God encounter and met Him, but have never pressed into becoming intimate with Him.

Why do so many Christians fail to experience intimacy with God? It's simple: Some Christians have no desire to become intimate with God. They are just looking for Him to give them eternal life and to be there when they need something. Others are just spiritually lazy.

Intimacy with God is not automatic. It takes effort and commitment on your part. God will not push Himself on you; He is like someone we see as being an introvert. Most of us have known someone that seemed a little standoffish, but once we work to develop a relationship with that person, we discover how much we enjoy him or her and what wealth of character that person has. I'm not trying to take away from the deity of God. He is relentless in pursuing you, but He also wants you to pursue Him.

James 4:8 says, "Draw near to God and He will draw near to you." Do you see where the initiative is? As we draw close to God, He draws close to us. It takes an unquenchable hunger on our part that says we are not satisfied with knowing about Him; we want to be intimate with Him. Jeremiah 29:11–13 says, "'For I know the plans I have for you,' declares the LORD, 'plans to prosper you and not to harm you, plans to give you hope and a future. Then you will call upon me and come and pray to me, and I will listen to you. You will seek me and find me when you seek me with all your heart'" (NIV).

Now, God did not say to seek Him through religion, through books, or even through experiences. He said seek Him with the *entirety* of your *heart*. The heart is the center of all human life; it is the organ that pumps blood throughout every cell in our bodies, bringing life to those cells. But it is also the center of all spiritual activity. Proverbs 4:23 says, "Keep your heart with all diligence, For out of it spring the issues of life." It is with our spiritual heart that we are saved.

The apostle Paul wrote, "If you confess with your mouth the Lord Jesus and believe in your heart that God has raised Him from the dead, you will be saved" (Romans 10:9). The heart—or the soul— is the seat of all our emotions. The shape of a heart signifies love; it is the symbol for Valentine's Day. Our emotions are a form of communication that convey what we are feeling inside; we express love from our hearts. Jesus said in Matthew 22:37, "You shall love the LORD your God with all your heart, with all your soul, and with all your mind." When the desire for intimacy with God is birthed, our love for Him and the depth of our intimacy is determined by the degree of love that we express toward Him.

Intimacy with God doesn't happen overnight. It takes commitment on your part to spend time with Him. I have heard of times when a prisoner and a person "on the outside" communicate by letter and maybe even visit from time to time—and sometimes these two fall in love. This happens even though they have never dated and have not had any kind of physical contact. They talk the chaplain into marrying them, and even though their marriage license gives them all the rights of a married couple, they do not experience physical intimacy with each other.

Intimacy with God is based on receiving Christ as our Savior and entering into a covenant relationship with Him. We often refer to this as having a *personal relationship with Christ*. I don't believe it becomes a personal relationship until we begin to spend time with Him, getting to know Him, knowing His heart and His will, and recognizing His voice. In a strong marriage relationship, we have an overwhelming desire to be with our mate. We should be jealous of our mate's time, wanting to have quality time alone with him or her. It is the same way with God; He is jealous over us and those things that steal His time with us. We need to be aware of anyone or anything that keeps us from His presence. Intimacy is an overwhelming hunger to be with Him, and there is a void in our life when we haven't been. David, the one who God says was a man after His heart, said this: "As the deer pants for the water brooks, So pants my soul for You, O God" (Psalms 42:1).

You must begin to trust God before you can truly become intimate with Him. Psalms 34:8 says, "Oh, taste and see that the LORD is good; / Blessed is the man who trusts in Him!" Our intimacy with God begins with our introduction to Him, then progresses as we *taste and see* who He is through the preaching and reading of His Word, through worship, and through our conversations with Him. As we become acquainted with Him, we begin to trust Him. We develop trust in Him by the revealing of His character to us. We begin to realize that He is faithful, He loves us, and He is merciful. As we begin to trust Him, we are able to release our cares and our concerns to Him. You will never become intimate with anyone, including God, until you can completely trust them. In any relationship, when trust is broken, intimacy stops.

It is in intimacy where God reveals His desires and our destiny. Our hearts begin to know His heart without having to ask. Our ears begin to recognize His voice clearly, because we have spent intimate moments alone with Him. We begin to see with His eyes and know the vision that He has for us. It is intimacy that brings us into a oneness with Him and causes us to be an expression of Him.

Determine to spend some quality time with Him so that you might enter into that position of true intimacy and allow God to show you what He has prepared for you. First Corinthians 2:9 states, "But, on the contrary, as the Scripture says, What eye has not seen and ear has not heard and has not entered into the heart of man, [all that] God has prepared (made and keeps ready) for those who love Him [who hold Him in affectionate reverence, promptly obeying Him and gratefully recognizing the benefits He has bestowed]" (AMP). Intimacy releases the goodness of God into our lives.